Everything You Want to Know about the Mission Field, But Are Afraid You Won't Learn until You Get There

Letters to a Prospective Missionary

Charles Troutman

InterVarsity Press
Downers Grove
Illinois 60515

Klaus de. Wilhelm

1977

Second printing, December 1976
© 1976 by Inter-Varsity Christian
Fellowship of the United States
of America

InterVarsity Press is the book
publishing division of Inter-Varsity
Christian Fellowship, a student
movement active on campus at
hundreds of universities, colleges
and schools of nursing. For
information about local and regional
activities, write IVCF, 233 Langdon
St., Madison, WI 53703.

ISBN 0-87784-717-7
Library of Congress Catalog
Card Number: 76-4738

Printed in the United States
of America

To my fellow worker
W. *Dayton Roberts*
who patiently sharpened the issues
of the changing face of missions
for a latecomer to the field

Contents

Introduction

My wife and I became foreign missionaries after age fifty not because we volunteered but because we were asked. We were not strangers to the missionary enterprise for we had helped promote missions for almost thirty years through Inter-Varsity Christian Fellowship and had had continuing contact with international students. But the possibility of becoming missionaries had been deliberately dismissed twenty years before. At that time we were already too old and therefore ineligible.

When we actually arrived in Costa Rica with the Latin America Mission (LAM), it was not exactly as we anticipated. It was harder to learn the language and understand the culture than we expected. We saw some mission attitudes we thought had passed out of existence a half-century ago. We discovered in ourselves unconscious, deeply imbedded paternalism. It was incomparably more difficult to present Jesus Christ than it had ever been in university discussions, and, strangely enough, our concept of the "mission field" had to be completely revised because of the strong family resemblance between the North American and Costa Rican cultures.

Then in two sessions of Inter-Varsity's Overseas Training Camp we could see that today's North American university students hold a missionary image even farther removed from reality than our own. Most felt that the very nature of missionary work requires North Americans who are domineering,

paternalistic and individualistic. They further assumed that
most of us had come to the mission field because we could not
make it in North American society. One student expressed
these preconceptions and changed understandings when he
said, "Why, I've found missionaries to be very intelligent!"

Now that we are on the field two attitudes strike us and
worry us. One, revealed in questions from friends, indicates
that the North American image of the missionary confines him
to a nineteenth-century role and is far removed from late twen-
tieth-century reality. Young people—the potential missionary
force—grow up sharing these attitudes for they know no others. At the same time they are in tune with changing tempos
and as a result their interest in a possible involvement in missions is subjected to serious question. How can students today
possibly consider fitting into an antiquated missionary mold?
I think we missionaries are responsible for this confusion because we find it easier to tell what we know an audience wants
to hear than to risk telling the story as it is.

The letters that comprise this book are written from real,
not imaginary, situations. The specific requests for help mentioned have been made by national leaders. The men and
women who have asked these questions are actual people
searching for their place of service for the Lord.

The term "missionary" is used in this book even though it
has some negative overtones. To some Roman Catholics the
term is associated with the more shameful aspects of the Spanish conquest. To Latin evangelicals it can imply that they
really cannot do the job on their own. Nevertheless, from a
North American perspective it is the best term to describe this
vocation.

In a way which I never discovered, John and his wife Carolyn, the main focus of these letters, became interested in
missionary work and wrote to several boards in the United
States. Because his desire to develop his pastoral ministry did

not fit into any of the immediate opportunities listed at the LAM office, John was urged to write directly to the field and to me as personnel coordinator. It may seem strange to most Christians that placing a pastoral missionary in Latin America is the most difficult assignment of all, and for this very reason I have chosen John as my example. The fact is that nationals are doing a far better job of evangelism and pastoral work than all but a handful of missionaries. On the other hand, placing a radio technician, teacher, nurse, camp director, theological professor, agricultural expert, university worker or community development agent is a relatively simple matter in modern missions. The LAM has attempted to adjust to this changing missions scene.

"Instant Decapitation" was the title given to an article written by Dayton Roberts describing the restructuring of the Latin America Mission into the Community of Latin American Evangelical Ministries which began to take place in 1970. This new structure, referred to in these letters as the Community and the context from which this book comes, is the reality out of which new relationships have developed for today's missionary. The term "community" is in common use in Spanish. It does not refer to the communities which have recently arisen in North America and Europe as part of the charismatic revival or the counter culture. It represents the restructuring of the LAM in more ways than one.

The reasons for restructuring were not exactly startling. There was no coup, no revolution, no organized protest. The organizational structure and administration were simply becoming inadequate for the expanding work. Instead of resolving the situation in North America, the Board of Trustees wisely asked for a consultation in Latin America. Most of the group were Latin Americans, many of them from outside the organization. They came together to answer the question, "What type of organizational structure is best suited to carry out the purposes of the Mission and is most congenial to the Latin American scene?" The simple answer, which reflects Latin attitudes toward development, was *autonomy in partnership.*

This conclusion was arrived at with considerable emotion not always understood by North Americans and was the basis of change from "Mission" to "Community." The former departments of a North American foreign missionary society became a federation of Christian service organizations located and organized in Latin America. The two North American organizations, the Latin America Mission of Canada and of the United States, are now fellow members of the Community. Their particular contribution is to offer the resources of more affluent societies to fellow believers in Latin America.

The eight former departments of the Mission became independent, legally constituted Christian organizations in the country of their major operation. It was understood that the majority of the members of their individual Boards of Directors would be Latin, although North Americans would not be excluded. These men and women would commit themselves to the same expansion of the gospel and the same theological basis as the North American Board. An international committee consisting of representatives of all these reorganized departments (plus other groups which have since joined the Community) was set up for coordination.

This change was not an accommodation to nationalism nor an expression of racism but a recognition that citizens of every country of both Americas have mutual responsibility for evangelizing this hemisphere. As a result, missionaries are no longer assigned to their work by a North American body but are invited to serve as qualified individuals by the leaders of Latin American Christian organizations. We are seeing that the unconscious distinction between first- and second-class citizens has been removed. All parts of the Community have become financially responsible instead of falling back on the old philosophy of "the Mission will make up any deficit." We are seeing a tremendous variety of creative growth limited only by the vision, capability and financial resources of the individual entities. Administrative limits are no longer set in North America. Decision-making is in the hands of those responsible for following through, and we are looking to Latin America for an increasing amount of support for the work. The Community, though it includes North Americans, is Latin in leadership, Latin in operation, Latin in responsibility and Latin in vision.

The letters that follow come out of Latin America and as such have a background of the historical Iberian domination of the continent. With the exception of certain Indian areas, the Latin culture is an offshoot of Western European Christian culture. The domination, paternalism and colonialism which have unfortunately been part of the Western missionary effort in the last two centuries, have not been limited to Latin America. While this book reflects the changing relationships of the missionary to his Latin coworkers, the principles are just as applicable in Asia and Africa because of the common factors seen in the emergence of the Third World since 1945.

I want to thank my secretary, Esther Rowe, who has shown unusual patience, my wife, Lois, who has been my chief sounding board and my fellow missionaries, who have sharpened the vision. I have learned from the students at the Spanish Language Institute in San José who have demanded answers to questions they did not know to ask before leaving North America or Europe. My greatest debt is to the Latin American leaders whose churches and work I pray will continue to grow. They have helped me see the missionary enterprise as both a necessity and a liability.

Letter 1

Are
You Sure
I Am
Wanted?

Dear John,

"Do the national churches really want me?" That is a perceptive way to ask about missionary service! You show a sensitivity not often expressed by North Americans. Such an inquiry never occurs to most people, even to many missionary leaders. They feel that this would question the Great Commission. Thank you for putting it so maturely.

Your letter and a note from the Mission Office in the United States came this morning. I could reply to your question quickly with both a yes and a no, but this would only confuse you. To expand the *no* first: There are places in this part of the world where nationalism of a particular kind is so strong that foreigners are simply not welcome in the churches. It makes no difference whether they come from North America, Argentina or Mexico. This may strike you as very unchristian, but you must understand what these people have been through. For generations they have been under foreign domination—first colonialism and military conquest and more recently an economic and industrial subjection. Can you understand that the growing attitude of independence touches the religious field as well as all others?

At the same time there are other areas where you, as a missionary, will receive a genuine welcome, though a big fuss won't be made over you. Your commissioning service in your own church will probably be the last time you will be the center of attention. The Community has a low profile in this part of the world, something quite different from the romantic concept you may have picked up. You will be accepted here simply as a person, working alongside national leaders who in some areas will have superior qualifications, and you will be evaluated on your ability to make a contribution to the local work. You will have no particular advantage or prestige because you are a foreigner. You will have to prove yourself just as you would in North America.

But for your own satisfaction you need to know more. You need to know why these openings exist. Sometimes the older tradition of foreign leadership so dominates that the national churches request more and more missionaries to fill the openings created by a growing work. "There is so much to be done and the missionaries can do it best." A student group asked for help in preparation for a series of evangelistic lectures. When it came to organizing the personal work, the leader very carefully explained the local situation. He felt students should not do individual witnessing: "You should organize the missionaries. Evangelism is their work, not ours." In such situations you will receive a royal welcome. But not all situations are like this.

The following personnel, either Latin or North American, are specifically requested by some part of the Community:

1. Two teachers to provide primary school crash courses for newly converted teen-agers who have not gone beyond second grade and are ashamed to go to school with seven-year-olds.

2. A Bible/theology teacher to train high school students, lay pastors, evangelists and deacons at a more advanced level than many pastors can handle at the moment.

3. Three nurses to operate rural dispensaries and to evangelize in connection with the local churches.

4. An agricultural expert for remote places where government help is unavailable.

5. A literacy expert to help believers learn to read the Scriptures.
6. A coordinator for a theological extension program.

These requests are all for rural areas. I have not included the urban list with openings for teachers, community developers, professors, radio experts, social workers and child care specialists. This list partly answers your question. The Latin church does want help. But if you look carefully, you can see that no position *requires* a North American. You will probably be in competition with national brethren for these posts and if they are available, you can guess who will be chosen. So, whether the Latin church wants *you* is an individual question that will take some more exploring.

It is proper to ask who drew up this list because it makes all the difference in the world whether the list of personnel needs represents the strategy of missionaries or the vision of the national church. I have seen lists prepared without anyone even talking to national leaders. Such an attitude presupposes of course that missionaries know what is best. But it is fatal for the mature development of the church and it is deeply resented.

This is our situation. The Church Association here is an independent, self-governing and self-supporting body, although historically it grew out of the activity of the Mission. Several years ago the Association requested a missionary to work under the direction of its permanent committees. This man has since been elected a member of the Executive Committee of this Church Association. He does not represent the Community or its administration nor is he expected to be a liaison. He was elected by virtue of his own personal qualifications. He shares in the work of the committees and in the general meetings of the Association. One thing he did was to find government statistics and United Nations reports which helped in planning. His participation in no way hinders the national leaders from working out their vision. They know their own situation, their resources, their pastors and their men in training.

Now I happen to know that this missionary has different ideas of needs and priorities of this denomination than do some on the committees, and he has done his best to promote them. But he recognizes that he looks on the scene from a North American point of view and in some areas he was scratching where it did not itch. This foreigner makes his contribution to the discussions, provides an outside evaluation and is able to have a proper influence, but in no way is he decisive or authoritative.

For you, coming here under such an arrangement would not mean that you would be a passive employee of the Church Association. After you became familiar and gained confidence, you would be expected to bring to bear all the ideas and insights you have. Your contribution would provide an additional perspective for the Association, but no authority or status would derive from your being a missionary. And, of course, you would be expected to contribute to the success of all adopted policies.

As I look at the area from which this list of needs is drawn, I can see opportunities for about twenty foreigners—teachers, pastors, professors, church planters, radio men and others. But my image of the Christian community also originates in North America and is not necessarily shared by evangelicals here. In fact, these people are building a different type of church in their society.

You are not only needed but urgently desired. But under two conditions: First, that you come qualified to fill a need recognized by the national leaders; and second, that you work *with* and *under* the jurisdiction of the Association. This is not very different from the present arrangements in your own church.

Sincerely,
Charles

Letter 2

Imperialism:
Political
and
Religious

Dear John,

I have the uneasy feeling that my reply to your question, "Am I really wanted?" was not quite adequate. In talking to a seminary student here in San José today, I realized that you, of course, had asked from a North American perspective and that I had answered from a Latin one.

You may have read the book *Missionary, Go Home* by J. A. Sherer. I'm sure you are familiar with the anti-foreign political slogans in all parts of the world. We cannot avoid being influenced by this bombardment. Instinctively we know that there must be good reasons behind it. And so you raise this matter of whether nationals really want foreign help, which you consider missionary work to be. Am I right?

Now, all national pride and rationalizations aside, let's be realistic. These countries do not like the fact that North American companies own most of their raw materials. They are critical of the U.S. government's foreign policy and angry in the face of investments that take away billions more than they put in. They are fearful that the U.S. Marines may land in their own country next. They dislike the arrogance of some tourists —and I could go on. There are anti-American clichés that come automatically from the far left for political purposes, but one does not have to be a revolutionary to see the substance behind these slogans.

The United States is not the only object of antagonism. For

example, many Germans are thoroughly disliked for their clannishness and lack of interest in national development. Two generations ago the British were thought arrogant. And in colonial days the Spaniards were the scapegoats. And once you come here you will see that some Latin countries fear each other more than they fear the United States or Europe. National animosities are just below the surface and are very strong.

But there is also the person-to-person level. Many Europeans, Asians, Africans and North Americans live and work in the Latin American countries. Most of these people are free from legal restrictions and relatively free from prejudice. During a recent anti-American demonstration in Panama, a North American was talking with a Panamanian friend as they leaned against a wall on which was written the slogan, "Yanki, go home!" The North American pointed to the sign. His friend, with a look of incredulity, said quickly, "Oh, but you are not a Yanki. You're a friend."

This may seem completely illogical as you read this in your home, but it is not so strange here. What this Panamanian objected to was exploitation, invasion and domination. Anyone who is sympathetic, understanding and open, no matter what his passport may say, is welcome and in most areas welcome to stay permanently. But North Americans must be thick-skinned in reference to their own country. You are not coming here to defend its interests and its foreign policies nor to rationalize its racial turmoil, which is a sensitive point.

Having said all this, there may be some places where you will be discriminated against because of your citizenship. You may find yourself a second-class citizen. This is a new experience for most Anglo-Saxon North Americans.

But your original question may have arisen in a theological and not a political context. In your travels you have probably had to face anti-Americanism on more than one occasion and

have survived emotionally. From the way you expressed yourself, I see you have come to terms with the image of your government overseas and the common reaction to it in many parts
of the world. Not that the issue is ever really settled. It erupts
at the most unexpected times and can catch you off balance.
But to have already faced the matter gives you a real advantage.

The climate of today's opinion raises subtle questions about
the basic morality of missionary work. It is usually stated this
way: "It is a violation of human integrity to impose our religion
and culture on others." Of course this assumes that all reli-
gions and cultures are only useful rather than better or worse,
right or wrong. Actually, the proposition is put more vividly as
"forcing our religion down their throats." This climate is one of
the consequences of our widening anthropological knowledge
and the communications revolution, but it is not the whole
story.

The fact remains that at times the Christian religion has
been forced down people's throats. The Crusades and the Spanish conquest of America are prime examples. Even Protestant
missions have not always been innocent. From a Christian
standpoint there is no justification for this method. We have
no right to advance Christianity by unchristian means. We
are always to respect the individual as made in God's image
and not *force* anything on him. But I am still puzzled as to
why Abner Hale of Michener's *Hawaii* is accused of imposing himself and his religion on the natives. The facts, even
as Michener presents them, do not support this view. Here
was one man isolated from home by months of travel, unac-
quainted with the language or customs, required to support
himself without military force or economic power. Yet in a
matter of a few years he was able to convince the majority of
the islanders that he taught a better way. Surely this was
not imposition.

I find it interesting that few North Americans object to political or medical imposition. Politically, the democratic philosophy of the United States is theoretically required of nations which are receiving aid programs. Most North Americans support this. Medically, the forced immunization of whole nations is seen as a good thing. Insecticides are sprayed over whole areas in completely arbitrary ways without concern for protest or concurrence. Even the most forceful of modern religious methods are mild by comparison.

As to this accusation of imposing a "foreign religion," let me make four observations which you may find helpful:

1. It is a sound ethical and biblical principle that the good things of life ought to be shared. Our Lord had strong words to say against those who refused to give of what they had to those in need. But it is more than that! To refuse to share is itself a sinful corruption as the Preacher declared, "There is a grievous evil which I have seen under the sun: riches kept by their owner to his hurt" (Eccles. 5:13).

2. We can truthfully say that most social scientists and anthropologists do not understand the New Testament faith and its implications and therefore will interpret the missionary situation very differently from the way a Christian sees it. They will make their scientific evaluation on the basis of social and cultural development without reference to or understanding of the supernatural dimension.

3. The role of the modern missionary is primarily to share his own experience of God's gracious love with those who know nothing of it. This is done both through proclamation and example. Missionaries should have no earthly empire to advance.

4. As believers we have no way of getting around the Great Commission of Matthew 28 and John 20. There are far greater issues at stake than cultural imposition or preservation. We are first citizens of God's kingdom and second of a kingdom

here on earth. We may even be called to go some places whether we are wanted or not. It is entirely possible that the Lord is
asking you to go through closed doors.

Sincerely,
Charles

Letter 3

Working with/under Nationals

Dear John,

Thank you for your reply to my letters. Please do not worry about a delay. Your days are just as full as ours. I am glad to do what I can to help your thinking now that, as you expressed it, "God seems to be moving me out of the home pastorate to overseas work." I will not comment on the way the Lord is leading as this is too personal a matter to discuss from this distance. Enough has been written on guidance to make it unnecessary to add anything. Your spiritual judgment can be trusted.

You raised the question, "If God is really calling me, how could I face a possible rejection, especially from national leaders who do not even know me?" Your theological problem really is, "Can my understanding of God's call be subject to the risk of human rejection?"

Traditionally, those who feel the overseas call apply to a missionary board whose duty it is to evaluate their spiritual, personal, physical, theological and academic qualifications. If all is in order, they are then sent out. Some boards give detailed assignments before the new workers leave their home country. In other cases boards send them to a specific field where they are then given definite appointments. Foreign missionaries and nationals are seldom consulted about these positions. They have already agreed to go anywhere and do anything asked of them. It might seem like a monastic vow. After all, how can they know at the beginning of their careers what the needs are or even what their own capabilities are? So you see, on various levels their "call of God" can be subject to frustration.

Perhaps this idea of total commitment to an organization sounds strange, but it has another side. The older type of missionary society has committed itself to the individual from acceptance to the grave. And without question this type of structure has been greatly used by God in the modern expansion of Christianity. Basic missionary decisions are made in New York, London or Paris. The boards send "shock troops" into pioneer situations. Missionary biographies tell their tremendous accomplishments. But this system has also entrenched the concept of benevolent paternalism which is producing such ugly fruit today.

In most mission societies, some fundamental decisions are made in mission home offices and others on the field. In the Community, decisions which will affect your life and work (apart from the screening process) are made on the field, not by field-based missionary administrators but by the governing bodies of the various national organizations.

So you see, no Christian structure, or any human organization for that matter, holds the answer to your question. Unless you work in a solitary way, you will always face the possibility of other human beings in authority making decisions which affect you. This is also true for you in the States. The change which has taken place here is that decision-making has been transferred from the home office to the field and on the field, from missionary administrators to all the leaders in charge of the local parts of the work. These leaders include both nationals and foreign missionaries.

Right now the members of the Board of Trustees in the United States are probably as much strangers to you as are national leaders. The time will come when you will know and love these Latin Americans and will develop a confidence and trust in them to a degree rarely possible with the Trustees.

We often hear today that "the age of missions is past." Some church leaders are so baffled by the radical changes taking place in the world that they see only one possible result—the disappearance of foreign missionary societies. This is already happening in some cases. But even if this so-called doleful prophecy should prove to be accurate, it is not true to say that the individual ambassador of Christ will disappear. He has been around for a long time, in fact for many centuries before the first missionary society was organized.

The Great Commission is not changing nor is the Good News nor personal responsibility for obedience nor the duty of churches to make possible the "going." It is the vehicle or apparatus for going that is changing. First it was the apostles then traveling evangelists then the monastic communities. In later times the vehicle has been immigration, conquest, merchant activities and royal decrees. And for the past 200 years the great expansion has come through organized foreign mission societies. Now pressures of world events are bringing new patterns.

Modern missionary publications all agree that missions have turned the corner in their attitudes toward total foreign domination. All boards are now committed to the indigenous principle of self-government, self-support and self-propagation, and emphasize the training and leadership of nationals.

But the outworking of this new attitude is varied. Some missions take all missionaries out of overseas work and nationals are left entirely on their own. Other boards turn over all work in a given country to national leadership but continue to loan certain personnel. In this arrangement missionaries are eliminated from a variety of responsibilities such as the pastorate, Sunday school teaching, committee membership and executive posts. Many loaned personnel find such a situation frustrating and without personal fulfillment.

The most common solution is the appearance of two parallel but independent organizations on the same field—the association of local churches and a continuing mission structure with a coordinating committee as go-between. This reduces missionary domination in the churches but at the same time prevents decisive national influence in mission decisions. There is a vast difference between listening to and submitting to national leadership. In this case missionaries continue to work with their own kind, trauma being at a minimum.

The Community took a bold step in organizing each entity in Latin America under Latin leadership. The next step was to make available the personnel—North American and Latin —as requested by each organization with no strings attached as to how this staff is to be used. In a few cases the chief executive officer is a North American, but only by choice of all concerned. Autonomy must not be limited nor its terms dictated from outside. The organizations are Latin, and there is no possible way of avoiding the fact of working under national leadership.

The theory is sound but the problems which affect missionaries are often emotional and psychological. (See Letters 12, 13 and 15.) We saw this very clearly a few years ago. One question on the Latin America Mission application form reads: "What is your attitude toward working (a) in full partnership with Christian nationals of the area you wish to serve; (b) under the direction of such nationals?" The Mission would not consider an applicant who was not unequivocally clear on this matter. One candidate replied, "I not only have no objections but would expect to do so as a Christian." Yet within a short time after restructuring he had returned to the United States saying that "all Latins are thieves; you can trust none of them; they can't keep their word; it's impossible to work with them, let alone under them."

You are perceptive enough to see that our structure would

place you under national leadership with no alternate option. There is no way to circumvent the policy and the reality. The step is as drastic as though, for instance, all Presbyterian functions had once been ordered by Scots in Scotland and at last had moved United States supervision to North Americans in the United States. You sense that there are many implications still to be worked out and that it is much more profound than the rearrangement of boxes on an organizational chart. Not all prospective candidates see the implications so clearly.

So you are right in understanding that the Board of Directors, the "Junta" we call it, of the Church Association has the authority to reject or accept and assign you as part of their team. If you were interested in seminary, school, hospital, student work, communications or any other ministry, the same possibility is there.

Yet your question as to whether you would have to work under nationals left me puzzled. I assume you feel that there might be other possibilities more attractive to you, such as working solely with North Americans or alone. In a few areas this might be possible. If you teach in a university you might be a lone wolf. There is always a possibility that missionaries may be serving on local committees and boards and in this sense you might be under some missionary supervision, but such a situation would be accidental. Of course, this ought not be the case if you decide to go with another mission.

But the simple answer is, "Yes, you would have to work under Latin Americans." Yet having just written this, I do not feel it gets to the root of your question. It is like saying, "Yes, you have to work under your presbytery or board of deacons." You feel at home in your present system. You know your own position and its web of relationships, and you speak the same language. In contrast you do not know the national leaders here and that makes you feel insecure. You have read about the culture but know this part of the world only as a tourist. You have yet to learn the language. If these things do not give you second thoughts, they should! But is this all that lies behind your question?

Let's face the fact that we North Americans come from a basically racist society. From our first steps we are taught that we lead the rest of the world—a thing we know almost instinctively. This is not just an Anglo-Saxon idiosyncrasy since North American blacks have similar troubles in Africa and West Coast Chinese are considered arrogant in Asia. We know there are "backward peoples" and "underdeveloped countries" and do not hesitate to classify them as such. You know as I do that North Americans feel instinctively that there are not many gifted Latins and that those few have self-defeating peculiarities. If we are not conscious of our subtle superiority, the rest of the world is.

You would feel much more secure if you could enter a North American organization, patterned along familiar lines and look forward to a working fellowship with like-minded fellow-citizens for the sake of the gospel in Latin America. But such a situation is changing all over the world. We needed a tremendous shifting of gears to make a missionary society which was effective in the forties adequate today.

Writing this blunt answer to your question on this glorious afternoon in the midst of this beautiful country does not seem to express the reality of serving Christ here. Let me see whether I can give another point of view. You will have a fascinating transcultural experience while seeing the Lord work under new circumstances and in different ways but with the same glory. Your own faith and love will grow deeper than you can imagine now. You will be privileged to work with men and women who will become your close friends, whom you will love and respect and who will contribute to your cultural and spiritual growth. Can you ask more of any position? All of us working here echo the words of Ken Strachan, a former director of the Mission, to a new candidate, "It will be fun working with you here."

Sincerely,
Charles

Letter 4

The Missionary Call

Dear John,

It is possible for airmail to reach us here in three days, but your last letter took a full four weeks. Our satellite progress has outstripped our postal services.

You expressed surprise that in my letters to you I have said so little about the "missionary call" itself. In fact, you wonder whether I am downgrading it and robbing missions of a theological basis. I believe that missions are grounded on a stronger foundation than only a subjective sense of God's call. The true basis lies in the sovereign will and love of the Creator God. But let me try to explain my hesitation in emphasizing the call in writing.

I recognize that some Christians place great significance on the meaning of a specific call received at a certain time and place. This certainly is one of the means which God uses to move some of his servants out of their own countries. And none of us should make a move overseas (or anywhere else) without the sense that the Lord is leading. Some even go so far as to consider a "missionary call" one of the special gifts of the Holy Spirit. But this, it seems to me, makes a distinction not required in Scripture.

My chief concern is with the overtones which have developed during the last two centuries around the idea of a "missionary call." Recently I overheard a new missionary tell his director that "God has called me to be a missionary to this country, and

only he can tell me what to do." Fortunately he retu
United States before he had a chance to become a
national pastors. I wonder what the present status ᴄ
is now that he is at home. The strong sense that the
call is a call of Almighty God has been the excuse for
ination and paternalism than we care to admit.

I believe that for all of us, those who can date th
those who can't, the real question is not so much tʰ
of a "missionary call" in itself as a step-by-steₚ
progressively developed over the years, even fron
In our early years a great deal of idealism and ad
be part of God's direction, but by the time we are re
the decision there ought to be a surer grasp of real
fidence in God's will for us. Part of this developi
will include a change from "I am called, therefor
thority to do thus and so," to "Here am I, help me tᴄ
ently."

In the last century there were probably very ₚ   a-
sons for emphasizing a general overseas call in   a
homeland call. The Student Volunteer Movement pieage card
made a special point of this. The success of this concentration is
a matter of record. But the latter half of the twentieth century
is a very different world. It seems strange to us now that such a
call must have a strong overseas flavor to make it valid—anywhere as long as it requires international travel. What is
wrong with a call to serve in a Chicago slum? Is it a lesser
place? For us the nineteenth-century "call" has no answers to
this question.

The major factor to affect missions, apart from the establishment of national churches, is the development of communications—radio, TV, transportation, linguistics, literature, sociology and so forth. Physically, no two places in the world need
be more than two days apart. The tools for service are fantastic
and improving constantly. So you see I am not so much inter-

ested in whether your "call" has an element of air travel in it and requires linguistic analysis but rather whether you are obedient to Jesus Christ no matter where you are. I believe you have already made this decision, and your work in the ministry is evidence. The geographic location and the language you use are not the major issues.

Look at your own situation. You have already served in an inner city church and now in rural Pennsylvania. If you stay in the United States, you can statistically expect to have four more pulpits before retirement. To move west of the Mississippi does not require a special kind of call. You have already made the basic decision. You only need guidance as to location. Now if you follow through the Lord's present pressures, you will require continuing guidance for possible service in places with such names as Nicoya, San Isidro, Cartagena and Sincelejo. You have already made the three great decisions of your life: salvation, vocation and marriage. The only thing I can do now is to present you with possibilities for service in Latin America rather than North America.

In spite of promoting missions all my life, I have always been uneasy about pushing a special overseas call. I do not find such a distinction in the New Testament. The gospel is for all the world. One statement of the Great Commission starts at home and ends at the far corners of the earth. The mission of the church is not determined by international boundaries or cultural barriers. Even in the early centuries the push toward expansion began in Jerusalem and spread inevitably toward Spain and according to tradition to India and Central Asia. Your home town is as important as Bogotá in God's eyes.

But, having said that, let's face the facts. There are tens of thousands of churches in North America, hundreds of Christian radio stations and evangelistic presentations and thousands of new books published each year. And in the rest of the world there are still 2.7 billion who have not heard of the Savior.

In spite of my hesitation to present a "missionary call," I have no hesitation in urging that you seriously consider joining us. I agree that you must not think of coming here without the confidence that this is his place for you, but I also insist that the "call" by itself is not enough. You would not move to a new pastorate on the sole basis of your personal conviction of being called without also receiving an invitation to go. Then you would visit such a church personally and pray through on the basis of all you know and see.

So you see that your description of our "overseas religious employment service" hardly fits the picture. Look at it this way: Of all the things which the North American church has to share with its sister church in Latin America, its dedicated members are more valuable than money or techniques. We can best share ourselves. Our programs and methods are often unsuitable. Our money can corrupt and control. We seek to be people-oriented rather than project-oriented. And we do this not in a general sense saying, "Here we are!" but in reference to a particular need in a particular place. These we call "Positions Available" or "Personnel Requests," and we explain the nature of each spot and may call it a job description.

In a business, industry or employment agency a job description tells not only what is expected and what training and experience is required but also sets limits on what can be done—a plumber must not interfere with the accountant. As one moves into the professional or management levels, the terms "position opening" or "job description" mean something a little different. At these levels the man makes his job not the job description the man.

In Christian service missionaries are more like these professionals. A Position Available means that there is a place in an organizational structure for a dedicated person. Of course he will have certain duties and responsibilities to perform and there will be a particular set of relationships. But what is expected from this person is that he will fulfill his work load and use this position as a launching pad for helping his fellow workers and creating new and different avenues for evangelizing and discipling. And this larger vision is exactly what will be expected of you as you fill one of these personnel needs. It is not worth all the effort of screening, selecting, securing support and sending a missionary just to fill a job description—no matter how badly needed or strategic it may be. There are simpler means of putting a live body into a slot. All this administrative detail, learning another language and adapting to a new culture are only worthwhile if the person fills his post explosively and carries his Christian witness into every possible corner. A Position Available is nothing less than this.

The listings of missionary needs which look so dry and statistical are far more comprehensive, more difficult and even more dangerous than you can dream now. I can appreciate your distaste for thinking of your missionary call in the same way as an electrician would approach an employment agency. You are right that far more is involved than qualifications, openings and contracts. We are about the same distance from you in Pennsylvania as you are from Denver. Why not come to Latin America and see for yourself? We would try to give you a broad exposure.

If this employment agency approach seems unspiritual to you, let me explain that its purpose is to realize one of the revolutionary changes taking place in the current missionary picture. It is this. Instead of being *sent* by a foreign missionary society to work in Latin America, you are now being *invited* by Latin Americans to serve with them in their own institutions.

Let me mention the pattern someone like yourself follows to see whther I can replace the agency image with the realities of the complete reversal which has come about.

1. The Community maintains a current list of requests for

help from each department.

2. You want to be used and sense a call to Latin America. You have already written about this.

3. The Board of Trustees in the United States looks into your spiritual, theological and professional qualifications before taking the responsibility for everything involved in your working outside the USA.

4. From the standpoint of Latin leaders, your call and acceptance in North America is not enough. They need to know more about you. For instance, the Church Association is very interested in two things: your professional qualifications and your personal evaluation of what you feel you have to contribute to the work. If they are satisfied, the Junta of the Church Association will then invite you to work with them.

We are not trying to squeeze you into the position most urgently needed at the moment, ignoring your qualifications and desires. We are trying to make it possible for you to find the place where you can use the special gifts God has given you. You are not assigned. You are invited, and it is your privilege to accept or reject the offer. This will become increasingly significant to you over the years. Do you see now the difference between being sent by a U.S. based organization to "impose our religion on the natives" and accepting a sincere request to serve in a national organization? If we appear to be an employment agency, it is to make this possible.

Sincerely,
Charles

Letter 5

Possibilities for a Missionary Pastor

Dear John,

The last few days have given opportunity to bring our list of personnel requests up to date. It is interesting to see the changes in just six months—some first-time openings, several old ones filled by individuals and missionaries who have been working in other areas, others filled by nationals and some eliminated by restructuring. Most requests for new missionaries take from two to three years to fill. By the time you are ready to take up responsibility, there will be additional opportunities.

You have given me the toughest job of all. If you were an agronomist, secretary, nurse, teacher, student worker, administrator or radio technician, I could offer you a choice of several openings. In the developing evangelistic thrust these are the areas foreign help is most often requested. But you are a pastor who wants to use your experience in Latin America. If only you were interested in seminary or institute teaching! Apart from these places, there are few openings. This may sound strange but not if you take the indigenous church seriously.

A generation ago many of the major pulpits were held by North Americans. Today only a very few are so occupied. Not only are there Latin pastors, but the church associations which have grown out of the work of the Mission are now on their own, independent of foreign administration and support. We thank God for this.

If we look at the role of the foreigner not from the standpoint of our overall purpose but strictly from the way each individual can be used, it is clear that this role is largely supportive. What we are trying to do, like the Apostle Paul, is to plant the motives and mechanisms for evangelism and discipling in each place—church associations, service organizations, youth groups, camps and other special activities. Then, as in the early centuries, the evangelism and development of each area become the work of the local believers. We must not forget that these activities must continue until the coming of the Lord. If their execution depends on transient foreigners, then the job is beyond us. The population growth alone will nullify our efforts. There must be some means of multiplying witnesses, not foreigners. Why should evangelistic responsibility be in foreign hands anyway?

Having said all this, you can see why there is no church open to you to pastor as there would be if you were to go to Seattle. This does not mean that there are no places for you. For example, there are twelve requests from national committees right now. This listing will give you an idea of what is open for someone with your interests.

1. One position mentioned before calls for a pastor/teacher to instruct laymen and lay pastors. This work would be a combination of pastoral counseling, teaching and training the leaders of about twenty-five congregations. Like Wesley, you would not be confined to any one. All are located in an agricultural-cattle area.

2. In a nearby country there are two requests to establish churches in large industrialized port cities among the more educated of the population. This is the group which tends to drift away from the churches. Your ministry would probably be first of all among high school and university students and their families. This is a very difficult area of pioneer work. You can see the possibility of a house-church ministry.

3. Most cities here include great masses of poor who have moved into the slums from country districts. They show all the disabilities of ghetto dwellers but having been newly uprooted are wide open to the gospel. Numerically, these folk present the largest challenge in Latin America, but so few of us know how to reach them. We have three requests in this area.

4. In inland areas there are a number of fairly large towns —fifteen to forty thousand inhabitants, centers of agriculture without evangelical churches. Several attempts have been made to establish groups in these towns, but they have failed. In the surrounding country there are some wonderfully alive churches composed largely of "peasants." The believers are very conscious of the social and educational differences between town and country (very few country pastors have more than primary education) although you and I would not be so conscious of them. The Church Association has asked specifically for foreign missionary church planters in five of these towns.

This does not exhaust the possibilities because there are many other opportunities which could be developed. But the church leaders feel that these requests are all they can make at the present time. They have very sensibly and honestly faced their own situation. They know how much they can absorb.

So while there are no longer churches for you to pastor, there are openings and requests for you to consider. But may I caution you not to read into these descriptions your North American situation. These are needs where no work exists at present. You will have no pattern or predecessor. You will fill a need, not enter a vacancy. This is pioneer work requested by the national churches.

Sincerely,
Charles

Letter 6

The Invading Army

Dear John,

In the more leisurely ways of our culture here we so easily forget the pressures under which you work. No apology is needed for your silence. Where you may be on call twenty-four hours a day, we here can take an hour and a half to cash a check or four hours to get a registered letter. We often envy the U.S. convenience of living.

I used the phrase "missionaries are more like professionals," and you asked, "More—than what?" Let me explain that I am not using the phrase in the sense of contrast between professional and non-professional missionaries, and it is important to see this changing role from a historical perspective.

The pioneers stand first. They were remarkable individuals and families, like the Moravians, whose biographies make exciting reading. Their work required unique personalities and has seldom been repeated. Many of them served beyond the limits of colonial control.

Then came the military conquest by Europeans of non-Western people and this coincided with the early phase of modern missions. Missionaries adopted the terminology of the military and spoke of themselves as an invading army—for Christ, of course. The mission station was an outpost in the midst of hostile territory, very like naval bases and cantonments of colonial powers. The heathen were the counterpart of the military enemy; potential candidates were recruits; natives were the submissive masses; backsliders were rebels. Native believers and native pastors were distinguished from the great missionary force. Their standing was certainly that of second-class citizens on earth regardless of their status in glory.

Missionary literature was (and often is) full of such phrases as "this couple is manning this strategic outpost," "they bore the brunt of the battle," "we must continue to hold this station," and "we must not retrench." The whole imagery was so military that "Onward Christian Soldiers" accurately reflects this thinking. The missionary was a soldier on foreign soil. Europeans did not seem to notice that this had quite different connotations for the victor and the conquered.

After the conquests came colonial governments to subdue peoples and exploit them for the benefit of the home country. The characteristics of colonialism are the presence of a foreign ruling group, a bureaucracy headed by foreigners and staffed by nationals, a residential compound, imposed laws, rules, regulations, communiques to the home office, furloughs, terminal appointments and so forth. Now just the listing of these words shows their striking resemblance to missionary terminology. Even the most spiritual literature carries these overtones. Missions shared the general concepts of colonialism—occupation, control and foreign direction. The missionary role was that of a member of a foreign bureaucracy even though his motivation was spiritual. Even today the term "old China hand" is applied to diplomat, soldier, businessman—and missionary. But let's not blame the missionary entirely. The whole structure put him in a position of authority, decision-making and superiority. Is it any wonder that there is a long history of resentment toward the missionary effort?

I have stressed this traditional colonial picture because in North America some still have this image of missions and missionaries. And there is considerable reason for this. We still think of "enlisting for life" to go anywhere and do anything that headquarters requires. Perhaps now it is without the heartaches caused by slow communication of the early days which made the whole effort a Protestant monasticism, but still our image is far out of date.

Just a month ago a visiting mission director objected to our professional concept as making control impossible. Of course professionals cannot be controlled! All that can be done is to set standards and provide the best possible framework in which to work. As though this director in Los Angeles could control new missionaries anyway! Within the past year I have come across the rules of several missions: permission to travel outside San José must be secured from the regional director in Honduras; for travel to Panama, from Chicago; United States income tax, social security, personal insurance and legal matters must all be handled through the New York office; salary payments can be made only by the U.S. office to a U.S. account; decisions on joint activities with other missions must be approved at the Columbus head office. How would you as a pastor in the U.S. react if your denominational headquarters acted in this manner? What room does this leave for the work of the Holy Spirit as guide and for personal maturity and initiative on the field?

Today it is almost impossible to be a geographic pioneer although there are levels of society, subcultures and areas of thought still to be penetrated. The missionary is not a "soldier" because he has no supportive power structure behind him. The use of power of any kind is deeply resented by the powerless. And bureaucracies are disappearing because missionary institutions are either being dissolved or turned over to national leadership.

When I feel liberated in comparison with these early missionaries, I must remind myself that they represent a level of dedication, sacrifice and persistence, a consciousness of tremendous opposition and a degree of loneliness and suffering of which I know little. My criticism is of the early structures, not the giants of the faith. But while I have been critical of the entire colonial concept, in all fairness we must see that Christians were alert to make good use of this political and economic vehicle (which was by no means one hundred per cent evil) for the spread of the gospel. The contemporary missionary problem is that colonial empires have gone and the missionary enterprise must now find new structures to continue spreading the Word.

Naturally so much role-changing is a source of confusion which I sense in your letter. So many feel that if the old patterns are disappearing, then the missionary enterprise is ended. But this is not so! It only means that there are different functions. And I describe the new work of the missionary as that of a professional—not as a career or non-career missionary —but as a professionally trained person in the context of missionary activity, that is, one who contributes his specialty, his competence to the Christian community. He has been previously trained in, say, photography and later joins up with a missionary organization. He is then a professional photographer working overseas for a mission board. Just as you have gone to your church as a professionally trained pastor to do the work of a pastor (not a lawyer or dentist), so you may come to this part of the world as a professional.

You can see why the term "missionary" is not really appropriate here any longer. You will not come with the authority of a church or a mission board but will be an invited pastor (or engineer, teacher, social worker, student worker, farmer or radio technician) joining other believers in serving the churches and the local communities.

Sincerely,
Charles

The "Professional"

Dear John,

I see from your question that I have written about the professional in missions but have not said much about what the qualities associated with a professional are. Let me see whether I can describe such individuals.

A decade ago it was fashionable to divide mankind into inner-directed people who were motivated by the force of their own personalities and outer-directed ones who responded because they were acted upon. This is probably oversimplification, but I hope it is clear that the role of a professional person is that of the inner-directed man.

He is an initiator, a *self-starter*. He does not depend on the direction of others to carry out his work. But he is not a lone wolf. In fact he is probably so specialized that he must work in a team to get anything done. He is expected to do more than simply fulfill a job description. He does not say, "This work is not in my contract." He has not only a carefully worded statement of his activities and duties but, more important, a place in a structure which is primarily a set of personal relationships. His colleagues expect him to be responsible both for a share of the work and for a creative contribution.

He is *self-reliant*. Not every organization considers this a virtue, but the biblical, healthy-mindedness of the command to love others as ourselves is what I am writing about. He is not completely dependent on others for his own well-being although he will always seek fellowship and cooperation. He is not dependent on the organizational structure for his work because he will quickly develop more work than his original assignments ask of him. Neither does he say, "I cannot do this" when no one will cooperate or when there is nothing in the budget. In other words, his security, satisfaction and effectiveness do not lie exclusively in the way people react or how the organization is structured.

Self-education is continuous. This will take many forms, but the important thing is that the professional seeks it out and is disciplined enough to submit to continuous self-training. The demands of the new job do not have to be tailored precisely to his previous training. He feels that God has provided him with the gifts of a trained mind and an inquisitive nature which enable him to decide what needs to be done, how to prepare himself and how to do it.

He is *self-disciplined*. He does not need rules and regulations to insure that he does his work. He does not need to be controlled to keep from dissipating his efforts. He is not required to work a certain number of hours per week. He can order his days so that his work and private life are in themselves a creditable witness to Christ. This takes some doing. In other words, he can be trusted. The issue is not control and supervision but opportunity, encouragement and counsel. In the very nature of the case a professional will always be working with and under men who know less about his specialty than he. The professor of Hebrew is expected to know a great deal more about his subject than the head of the seminary.

Over half a century ago in Korea the well-publicized indigenous church used the phrases "self-government, self-support and self-propagation." This "three self policy" has been a guide for establishing indigenous churches around the world, but missionary societies have been reluctant to apply the same principles to themselves or their personnel. One consequence of this has been the running controversy and tensions between "mission" and "church" which is still largely unresolved, as you know.

We have taken the logical steps to bring the organizational structure and personnel policies into line with these principles of indigenization. It is a far more difficult path than a bureaucratic or hierarchical one as you can see. When we speak of the growing maturity of the national church through being indigenous, then these "professional" qualities are synonymous with Christian spiritual maturity on the part of the missionary. But the point I want to make is that the new role of the missionary will predominantly demand people with such qualities. The needs of Latin America, and especially of its Christian community, require that most missions move in the direction I have described.

There are openings requiring foreign help. One of these, as I have written, is for leadership in pastoral training in rural areas, and you are considering it. The new organization is now geared to present you with the opening for possible service because you are prepared professionally and, of course, spiritually.

I do not mean someone who is individualistic, but more like a person in industry or government, a faculty member in a university or a lawyer in a corporation. In such situations the professional has two loyalties—to the organization in which he works and to his own profession. In the institution he is expected to do a certain job and to fulfill other related responsibilities—faculty committees, special assignments and so forth. At the same time, he would be expected to carry out responsibilities to his profession as a member of various learned societies, in special research and writing and other activities which would contribute to the profession.

Your loyalty to your profession would include more than your initial qualifications. You should be an active member of and subscribe to the contributing journals of your profession, both in English and Spanish. You should contemplate study furloughs and seminars in North and Latin America and possibly Europe. Your library is important although book work is often a struggle in the tropics. All this is on top of your work with the Church Association. Does it seem too heavy? Perhaps so, but no more than we hope you are planning if you remain in the United States.

So you see that the needs of the next missionary generation require some forward moves where we have little precedent. A pioneer is heroic. The "general missionary" still has a place. The maverick is always interesting and challenging. A short-termer can bring freshness and energy. But the long-term need for the most part will lie with the man we call a professional. You are already in professional work and similarities between North America and this part of the world are greater than the differences.

Sincerely,
Charles

Letter 8

Your
Life
Work

Dear John,

"If we consider missionary work professionally as you describe, how can we possibly think of it in terms of a lifetime career?" You can't—although it may become your life work. It is really no different from your present situation. The fact that you responded to the call to the ministry does not automatically mean that you will remain in your present pastorate all your life. So it is with missionaries. The time may come when the need you were originally meant to fulfill will have been met. Then thank God for the success he has granted. I will be very surprised if, while you are serving in this pastoral work, you are not challenged by many different opportunities and pioneering areas of work into which you will long to move. You will wish you were twins. After fifteen years of teaching, one of our seminary professors saw the fantastic opportunities for Christian witness in local government service. A whole segment of the Christian community would not exist here today had he not left the seminary.

This new concept should have considerable influence on how you seek guidance. The issue is not a lifelong commitment to one limited area of work but a confidence that for the present the Lord is calling you to join a particular team in a foreign country to do a specific job. The one difference between this decision and an invitation to a pulpit in California is that you have to face the fact that here three or four years will pass before you feel at ease. This is not an insignificant factor, but is not very different from a decision to obtain a Doctor of Theology degree in Germany. Your life work is to serve the Lord. Where you serve may change a number of times.

Your letter of this morning asks for more discussion of a lifetime commitment and the possibility of a shorter period of foreign service. You are right in sensing that most Christians feel that missionaries should somehow, as in marriage, take a vow that only death breaks. Even retired missionaries are sometimes looked on as those who should be out on the firing line until the last heroic breath. If these folk are suspected of giving up too soon, what a dark cloud must hang over those who serve for only five, ten or twenty years! You know what I mean!

On the other hand, you wonder whether you could even make a decision for a ten-year span of your life involving a part of the world you know very little about, a culture which you may not find compatible and a group of leaders who are unknown to you. Humanly speaking it is ridiculous to expect you to make such a decision with such limited information. Your concern is certainly in order. Let me describe these three different factors more fully.

First, there is the language. If you have a normal aptitude, you will probably feel at home in Spanish in about four years, and if you continue to study, you should be relatively fluent in seven. If your language aptitude is low, it will take longer. This does not mean that you will have no ministry until you are fluent but that there will be a struggle with the language—an additional burden which you do not have in your present ministry.

Then there is the culture. An American anthropologist recently stated that it takes from five to seven years of living in another culture for even a specialist to understand it. Now if this is true for such highly trained people, what can we expect for ourselves? You know something of this problem from your ghetto work. An agricultural worker might be able to advise on improved farming techniques soon after arrival, but as a pastor your work must be at a much deeper level. If culture is defined as a means of intelligible communication, then you have a good deal of learning before handling the gospel effectively.

Perhaps the most weighty consideration is that expressed by David when he commissioned Solomon to build the temple. We are all of us "strangers and foreigners" and the task is great. We are "soon cut off" and others must rise up. One long life-time of service is not enough for the job at hand. The purpose of God in Latin America covers generations, and we need to think carefully lest we make the job too small.

Now in the light of these factors, I think that only God him-self can guide you. We do not ask you for a lifetime commitment —only that you weigh seriously the vastness of the task. Since the Lord seldom leads in more than one step at a time, this is enough. It is a far cry from clarity on a lifetime commitment.

In this context let me mention the self-supporting mission-ary. During the last generation the idea of a non-career mis-sionary has carried a glamor often lacking in the picture of the ordinary missionary. Those who saw opportunities for service outside the usual orbit of missionary activity or who felt that the regulations of missionary societies were irksome or who balked at having to raise their own support have found here a possible way of obeying the Lord's commands without tradi-tional shackles. In general a non-career missionary is one who desires to do missionary work but is completely self-support-ing. He may be employed in a government agency, foreign or local business or in the educational field. Many are bilingual and bicultural before they begin. They are already successful in overseas secular work when their growing spiritual matur-ity automatically leads them to be "missionaries." These quali-fications are held by very few.

But the limitations of this type of service have disillusioned many who have tried to serve the Lord this way. For example, they seldom begin churches or church associations because the demands of their full-time work and its social requirements leave little spare time. They face pressures from their employers which can be very demanding in a foreign context. The competitive field of business which has never had the tempering effect of a Christian conscience can be a liability to witness. If a person thinking about this type of service is not already successful in his own country and carrying a full load of effective Christian activity at the same time, there is little reason to suppose that he can make much contribution to the local cause of Christ in a foreign country. Most Christians require some structure and a built-in Christian fellowship to make a contribution in another culture.

On the other hand there is a tremendous need in the Christian community for just this type of person. His chief contribution to the cause will be his Christian witness in the upper levels of society. This is a worthy achievement in itself. He will probably be in a position to bring influence to bear on behalf of the Christian community in official circles. And he will be able to counsel local Christian groups in matters of business, legal and committee activities. Such work is often crucial for the ongoing cause of Christ. It requires a genius to handle all this, and the effective non-career missionaries I know are exactly that. In spite of the unusual demands of his situation, such a "missionary" is an important part of the task force of world evangelism.

But I want to turn the tables and ask you a question. It is loaded. Will you try to spell out your understanding of what you can contribute in Latin America to see whether it fits our expectation? Perhaps it will help if I explain first what I am not interested in.

I am not interested in your humility. This is a characteristic which is desperately needed, but none of us is wise enough to evaluate himself. You can be so humble that you give us no idea of your real capabilities. Let others evaluate your spirituality.

You may be willing to do anything or go anywhere requested of you. But if this is your honest attitude, then you are saying in reality that you are capable of tackling anything (with God's help of course) and everything which the unknown future may throw upon your path. Be careful! If you are not very clear here, you can fool yourself. It is much easier to imagine rising to the tremendous spiritual demands of the future than to analyze your present capabilities. You are confident that you can trust God in all kinds of crises in the future, throwing down principalities and powers and triumphing over impossible circumstances through mighty faith. And may it please God that this is exactly what will happen. But this is not the question.

The thing I really want to know is what you think you can contribute to the work of Christ in Latin America. Or, to put it a little more sharply: What contribution do you think you can make as a foreigner in one of the situations I have previously described?

We have surveyed the whole area and have long-range plans. I will try to mesh your desires and capabilities with this vision. Your reply to my question must be in the light of this perspective. I will be very interested to hear from you.

Sincerely,
Charles

Letter 9

Using Your Preparation

Dear John,

I did not expect you to reply at such length but am very grateful for your thoughtful analysis. Your professional training in pastoral counseling shows through and gives insights that few candidates are capable of. Let me comment on those matters which seem especially significant.

I see your long description of God's call to this general area as part of his preparation in your life. This, of course, is as it should be and is the first step. But some people feel that nothing more is involved. One accountant was in such a hurry to answer the call of God that he wanted us to teach English to his potential coworkers so that he could practice "instant obedience."

Then you feel there is a job to do here which you are capable of handling. And because of your restlessness in North America, you have looked around and discovered this appealing situation. You also express a feeling that this bicultural experience should be good for you. This also is as it should be. Latin America has much to contribute to the personal development of us all. In addition this shows a sense of personal longing for a deeper spiritual and personal fulfillment than appears possible where you are. My only concern is that you make very certain that your restlessness is not simply a desire to run away from your present situation.

You have certain ideas on pastoral counseling and church

growth. Call them a theology of evangelism or of the church, a psychology of counseling, a philosophy of education or any other academic name. These ideas are bound to be modified in a different culture, but I am pleased to see your eagerness to experiment and develop them in a completely different situation. I think you already sense the need for balance between imposing your ideas on a new culture and coming into this situation completely blank. There is just one word of caution. Don't limit God to your present interests. Perhaps they are only preliminary. Under a different sun in a new culture with a new language, he may give you an interest beyond anything you can now dream. May I thank you again for your thoughtful reply.

But do I detect in your letter some question as to the wisdom of burying your life in one of the more remote sections mentioned? This is a proper question for you to ask at this stage. I am sure that if the Lord himself pointed out clearly to you one of these tiny spots on a map, you would go gladly. You are not unwilling to obey, but not being certain of his direction, you question the possibility of your own personal and professional development. Since this is often one of God's avenues of guidance, your hesitation is valid.

Let me describe what your situation could be like in one of the country towns I mentioned previously. I do this because these openings are the most complex, the hardest to describe, the most unresponsive so far and the most difficult to adjust to culturally and climatewise. Yet these are strategic towns in a developing section of the country. The job requires the talents of a considerably more than average person who has the intelligence to understand the situation and the ability to act.

These country towns by North American standards are very primitive. Yet they have good access to the large cities and serve extensive areas. You would have the support of rural churches in the area and some sympathizers in the town. We

feel that a foreigner should take no more than four years to
establish a church. To stay longer could result in over-depen-
dency. You can visualize all that is involved in a congregation
much better than I, so I will not say more.

You would not only be a church planter and developer. One
of your most important roles would be living as a Christian in
this community. You might be the best educated and most
widely traveled person in miles. And just as your present
church does not exhaust your opportunities for Christian witness, so there will be open doors on all sides, even in the midst
of traditional opposition. Actually your problem after the first
year will be priorities—how to divide your witness between the
church and the community.

The following list suggests the kinds of opportunities you
could find:

1. You and your wife can offer to teach in one of the schools,
perhaps only conversational English at first.

2. The local radio station is crying for something more than
advertising. Until you become fluent, you will have to speak as
a foreigner but may be able to give your observations on sex or
family problems. You may have a course in English conversa-
tion, using the New Testament as a text. However, you should
not try to be an evangelist or pastor on the air until you have
mastered the language, syntax, vocabulary and phonetics.

3. There will be citizens' committees you can join although
fewer than the number you are used to.

4. Bible discussion groups seem to be popular among the
more educated, and your wife Carolyn could have a special
ministry with the women.

5. You could organize a school for teen-age dropouts who
have recently been converted.

6. There are dramatic and literary clubs in some of these
towns.

7. Public health services are always in need of help in pro-

moting ideas. Of course, the larger the town, the more opportunities, but a consecrated imagination can take you a long way. Your contributions may be very small, at first, but these activities are the quickest way to understand and become a part of your adopted country.

You will find a wider variety of areas for personal development and involvement in this situation than in North America. Your church may not become known as a center for pastoral counseling, but you can be useful as a man of God in diverse situations. And as you gain experience and fluency in the language there will be calls on your ministry from all over the region.

What I am trying to explain is that your pastoral counseling experience will be extremely valuable but in quite different ways. If you are thinking in terms of a long pastorate where you may give leadership to a growing congregation over the years, then this type of opening is not for you. But if you think in terms of doing what no national pastor is able to do now because of lack of preparation, if you are prepared to build up to a position into which he may soon step—and probably do a superior job—then you are enthusiastically welcome here.

The opportunities are tremendous, and the Lord knows what the needs are. You have very little to contribute as a North American, but as a specially trained brother in Christ you have much. And I think the opportunities are more obvious here than where you are at present. I hope you won't tire of my emphasis that your task is to know where the Lord wants you to go.

Sincerely,
Charles

Letter **10**

A Dozen Successors

Dear John,

I am glad you saw the connection between church planting under the authority of the Church Association and the new role of the missionary who is a professional. We are not empire-building, or, more accurately, we are not feathering our own nests. When you see these rural towns you will understand why the symbol of empire is inappropriate. There are few feathers.

But then as an expression of this new role you quoted the famous saying, "A missionary should work himself out of his job." This slogan was first used in Korea at a time when the missionary enterprise looked as solid and permanent as the other institutions of that day—the British Empire, the Cunard Line, the Austro-Hungarian Empire, the undisputed superiority of Northern Europe and America and so forth. In Korea there was Nevius and in India Allen who saw through the weakness of building spiritual work on colonial structures. At a time when the progress of Christian missions was expected to go unchecked, this slogan struck at complacency like a thunderbolt. The slogan said that the church was not the property of the West but of Jesus Christ and the local believers. And it was a missionary who first suggested that he "go home."

But I hate this slogan of "working oneself out of a job." It can sound like an apology for a dying enterprise. In the face of the needs of the world, it is negative and an expression of retreat.

It is out of keeping with the aggressive commands of our Lord. Worst of all, it suggests that we don't have to come to long-term grips with God's assignment and robs missionaries of the vision and hope they should have. And to candidates like yourselves it shouts that if the task is not to your liking, you can maneuver in such a way that you can go home without losing face by telling your constituency that you have worked yourself out of a job. Thoughtful supporters may then wonder whether your involvement was a good investment of their stewardship.

Just the other day a fellow worker said to me, "When a national takes over my position I might as well go home!" What lack of vision! What a travesty on the world's needs! And he thought he was being biblical and holding a progressive missionary attitude. I had just finished listing some sixty positions that were open, a dozen of which he could fill.

I believe that the New Testament pattern for a foreign missionary is more than finding a replacement. He should work in such a way that he will leave more openings for service than there are people to fill them. He has no right as a servant of Jesus Christ to be concerned about only one successor. He should need a dozen. The biblical figure is not that of a soldier whose term of enlistment is finished as soon as there is someone to take his place but of a sower who goes forth to sow thirty, sixty, one hundred per cent increase. Can the needs of men be met or the world evangelized by anything less?

Your dozen successors will not be in pastoral work alone. Your service will be broader than that. One of our most needed personal characteristics is flexibility. The traditional picture of a missionary is that of one who can do everything. If the pigs are dying, he knows what to do. When his car breaks down, he is the mechanic. When the accountant goes on furlough, he keeps the books although his most recent math may have been high school algebra. He is the preacher, the evangelist and the chairman of meetings. When a field administrator or theological professor is needed, he is assigned. If deputation is needed, he goes home for a period of time to raise funds. Nothing is considered too much to ask of him nor ănything unfair. But this "flexibility by assignment" is not what I am talking about. You can see this as a hangover from pioneer days when what the missionary could not do was left undone.

On the other hand the concept of a specially trained professional may appear to rule out automatically the need for flexibility. Nothing is further from the truth. It is a flexibility of a different kind. The Community is neither large enough nor wealthy enough to afford a specialist for every position, and we are always stretched beyond our abilities. Our resources never equal the need.

It is within this context of more openings than we can possibly fill and the speed of development that we see the need for flexibility. You will not come into a static situation. While you are serving within your professional sphere, you will move out into other areas in ever widening service.

For example, a professor of communications in the seminary offered to help form a committee of nationals to develop child care centers. After two years of committee work she was asked to serve as full-time coordinator of this venture. Almost one hundred nationals are now working voluntarily in the spiritual and physical care of children. This highlights the possibility of a complete vocational switch. In this case the missionary helped create a new position which she filled. She has now gone a further step and relinquished this position to a well-trained Latin American so that she can work on new developments in the organization.

A student worker gave his Sundays helping a struggling local church get on its feet to the point of having its own pastor and six elders although he himself would never have described his work as "church planter." In our original sense he did not work himself out of a job but created others.

You see what I mean by flexibility. You can experience a sense of deep personal satisfaction in learning to work effectively in areas you would not dream of touching in Pennsylvania.

Sincerely,
Charles

Letter 11

Living in Another Culture

Dear John,

You asked about life in our missionary compound. Although many missions still have compounds, we have none nor even a policy as to your living arrangements. Nevertheless, on occasions we see this traditional mentality. Recently two new missionaries were deeply disappointed that they could not become part of a spiritual, working, Christian ghetto. They felt that it was unspiritual to live just as we lived in the States—separated in various parts of the city. Our only problem now is that we have to be careful that too many missionary families do not move into the same neighborhood. On the principle that we consider you a professional, there are no housing regulations. You will not be told where or how to live any more than the Board of Regents of your university would tell a professor how to proceed. So upon arrival you will take your time to look over the situation and make your own decisions. Temporary arrangements will be made during your language study.

Originally compounds provided the protection, sanitation and living arrangements necessary to enable missionaries to get on with the job they went to do. In so many countries the mere job of living was more demanding of time and energy than foreigners were able to give. As a North American, wherever you are you will be isolated culturally to some extent—considerably at first, less later on. This is not your fault. You were just not brought up in Latin America. Identification at best will be incomplete. It will have to be a continuous, conscious and intelligent effort, at times amounting to a real struggle. Now you can see that a compound intensifies the isolation of missionaries from the local culture.

Psychologically and spiritually this means that in coming here you will not enter a closely knit supportive group ready to provide for your spiritual and social life. Of course you will not be ignored, but if you are counting on "compound life," it could be a disappointing experience. The modern mission field is not the place for anyone whose effectiveness depends largely on a supporting circle of friends any more than most vocations in North America. My reason for writing this way is that you will not expect something of the situation here that it cannot provide.

Isolation will be greater should you live in a rural town away from other kindred spirits. But I am thinking particularly of the growing concentration of missionaries in the cities because of population movements. Each has his own work and is fully involved, leaving very little time for socializing with one another.

We are neutral as to whether you rent, buy or build your home. Do as you wish. My wife and I purchased our own home and without realizing it stumbled onto an extra bonus. Several students said to us, "We are glad to see that you are taking this country seriously." Traditionally missionaries are prepared to endure the uncertainty of constant rentals because of long furloughs, frequent transfers and the desire to be mobile for Christ's sake. There are still those who need such mobility. But for decades in practicing this pilgrim ideal we have unfortunately said, "I work here, but my home is really elsewhere." We did not mean to say this. But in a new culture it is seldom possible to know exactly how our words and actions are going to be received and what meaning will be attached to them. Anthropology and sociology study these areas and explain why we are often surprised and confused.

For example the desire of early missionaries to be simple and unpretentious in dress led to the black suit, white shirt and tie becoming a sought after status symbol on the part of national believers. Spirituality could then be evaluated by how a man dressed!

In another area many countries are bound in an unbreakable poverty cycle caused in large part by an unrestricted birthrate. But any attempt at birth control aid through international organizations is understood to say, "This is the way rich nations try to keep us down."

The love and concern which we as Christians are commanded to show to those in need can be interpreted as a means of paternalistic control. Generosity can be considered a power play. Cross-cultural understanding in the context of your spiritual development can be one of the most intriguing aspects of your life here.

You have given clues about your image of missionary life. You envy us our close fellowship in the work and the things of God—something which you seem to miss in your pastorate. You wrote of working in a team, and in your last letter you spoke of contributing your share to the life of the mission family. Now in one sense you will find this fellowship you are looking for. But, as I have explained, there is very little of the "mission family" concept any more. We have grown away from it. Does this sound strange?

The Mission, even fifteen or twenty years ago, began to sense that if we were to work effectively, we would have to be more closely identified with local churches, and activities of the normal life of the country. Life was full then, so that to take on further responsibilities meant that something had to go. Slowly but surely time previously spent in "missionary fellowship" was drastically limited.

For example, the expanding camping program involved

more and more personnel at the time of the Annual Mission Meetings. One single mid-week prayer meeting for all members of the Mission became a physical impossibility in the face of claims from seminary, hospital, high school, local churches, radio station and other activities. Evangelism-in-Depth campaigns took a number of families to various Latin American countries. We have prayed for increased identification and usefulness among the people here and God has answered beyond our expectation. But in the process there is much less time to enjoy fellowship with our missionary coworkers.

Your immediate reaction may be, "At the cost of spiritual deterioration!" But you will find that God is requiring a creative trust and dependence in ever more complex situations. Instead of the one weekly prayer meeting the week is full of departmental and small group meetings for Bible study and prayer which meet a wider spectrum of need and opportunity than was ever possible under the old "one family" system. It is stretching us but God is faithful.

In this present situation you will gather your own circle of friends, some Latin Americans, some from the Community and some foreign residents. Your closest friends may not be fellow missionaries. But you can count on God to give you close Christian fellowship and support in the circle of friends of his choosing rather than having it artificially controlled through compound life. The idea of a spiritual community for mutual growth and action seems to be an idea which is very congenial to the Latin culture. The Lord is using such communities increasingly. But this is no different from your accustomed pattern of life, and you know how God has used these friendships in your own personal maturity.

Sincerely,
Charles

Letter 12

The Missionary's Family

Dear John,

Your question about family, especially your children's education, and about what your wife will do, came at a good time. During the last few days I have been involved with a large group of new missionaries in language school representing a dozen different societies who are working their way through problems of culture shock. The adjustment seems more acute for North Americans than for Europeans and is something which cannot really be faced prior to entering a new culture. There is something about the sheer size of the United States and Canada that insulates our imagination so that we cannot prepare ourselves for the experience. Europeans are much closer to other cultures geographically than we are. Since culture shock catches most missionaries by surprise, it can be faced only after the attack has begun.

Concerning your children's education, the decisions seem very complicated in another country. In reality there is no single pattern. Six different points of view came to light in our discussion.

1. Some believe that a Christian school education is as much a spiritual requirement as church attendance and Bible study. This means leaving children in the U.S. or finding a mission boarding or day school.

2. Some feel strongly that anything in North America is superior to anything they can obtain elsewhere. This often

means leaving children with relatives for their high school education.

3. Others want to take full advantage of living in a new culture by giving their children an education in the local schools—in Latin America this usually means a private school. Two of the best here in San José are German and French so that children may become trilingual. There are other schools based on the North American educational system.

4. Others want to play it by ear and do what they feel best for each child.

5. Some parents prefer to be responsible at least for the primary education of their children through home study courses under the mother's supervision.

6. Finally there is also that very common attitude that the work comes first—God will take care of the children and the plans for schooling are not considered important.

We feel that we have no authority in such a very personal matter and leave each couple free to follow its own convictions. It is my own feeling that your location at the various stages of your family's education will determine your decisions more than anything else. Also the quality of primary and secondary education is being improved rapidly in most countries so that the desperate need to send children to North America or to boarding schools on the field is not the issue it was twenty-five years ago.

Education today in Latin America is different from that in North America but not necessarily inferior. Just as some education in the United States is patently poor, so it is in parts of all countries in Latin America. So you see that in the midst of many factors, you will be free to decide as you think best. Raising your children biculturally can be one of the greatest privileges of their lives.

In missionary circles it is increasingly evident that one of the greatest contributions a Christian couple can make is to raise a Christian family in the midst of another culture. After the "Communist liberation" of China, I heard an experienced missionary tell a student group: "We now feel that one of our great deficiencies was in the area of the Christian home. We sent our children at an early age to missionary boarding schools and saw them only during vacations. Of course we were free of family duties and could carry on our work in a way denied Chinese pastors. But the Christian Chinese families rarely saw a foreign Christian family in action. We demonstrated sacrificial service, personal witness and devotion to duty but never the thing they needed most to see—a Christian home in a non-Christian culture." One missionary child who completed high school on the field and is now in a large state university in the United States said recently, "I would not trade anything for the special privileges of my bicultural education."

In the culture shock conference I referred to in the beginning, the visiting psychologist emphasized again and again that stability for most children lies in the home rather than the school. School seldom provides solutions for a child in trouble or the motivation to take advantage of the opportunities. The Community makes every effort to cooperate with the educational desires of each family, and the experiences of the various families in a given location can serve as a very helpful guide in the first choices. Familiarity with one's new home and the opportunities for local education can then clarify or modify that original choice.

There have been big differences of opinion on what the wife is expected to do. Will you forgive me if I take the long way around to answer your question?

Traditionally the Roman Catholic solution to the problem of Christian service and the family has been celibacy. Not that this is the origin of the doctrine, but the fact that priests and nuns are completely free to devote full time to the service of the

Church has been a significant factor. St. Paul speaks of the freedom of single persons, widows and widowers. The Reformers (not holding to celibacy) broke the custom, but we Protestants have never been able to escape the idea that family life somehow interferes with God's service. Now no one will question that a family does make considerable difference and that it often requires profound restructuring of work patterns. Because of this most missionary organizations have tried to reduce family interference to a minimum.

The most common device was to require that children be sent to boarding school at an early age. Another was to consider wives full-time missionaries as well as husbands and to expect full-time work from them in spite of pregnancies and nursing periods. The wife's assignment could be so completely different from her husband's that they had little opportunity to work as a team. Some of these practices are still common. Strangely enough, many faithful supporters feel that they are not making a profitable investment if the woman is "only wife and mother." They want two for the price of one.

We have come to look at this matter differently. We feel that the biblical description of a married couple being "one flesh" should be taken seriously in our personnel policy. We also feel strongly that father and mother have a supreme responsibility toward their children. Yet acknowledging these two principles, there are many variations. For example, some wives feel that as long as their children are living at home they should be full-time homemakers. Others feel that during school hours the wife can be involved in some work outside the home. Still others feel they can handle both full-time responsibilities. We will not decide how you as a family should develop your involvement.

You will have to make this decision before the Lord. We can give you an idea of the possibilities. You will have coworkers who feel that every wife should be employed full-time in missionary work, and certainly many from other mission societies will feel this way. You can expect some pressure in this area in spite of our official policy.

My own impression is that your wife will find a greater variety of activity here in Latin America than she now finds where you are. As I mentioned concerning your own work, after the first year your decisions will revolve around priorities.

I'm also enclosing a letter from my wife. I thought she could give a good perspective on some practical aspects of living overseas.

Sincerely,
Charles

Letter 13

Practical Adjustments for the Wife

Dear Carolyn,

Would a woman's point of view be helpful at this stage of your thinking? Men react in one way to basic changes. Sometimes our responses are very different—more subjective and more emotional. This won't be an essay, just a series of unrelated but, to me, significant adjustments.

Because of the complications of daily living—food preparation, matters of hygiene, and others and the fact that it is unwise to leave a house untended, you will probably need live-in household help. Lots of adjustments here—some pleasant, some tedious and many humbling and confusing.

One of your big jobs will be to make this new culture completely "home" for your children while keeping ties with North America warm and real. Their later reaction to missions and even to the Lord will depend in large part on you.

Happily this experience has clarified priorities on the value of "things." What one leaves behind or misses at first is soon replaced with interest in new cultural expressions. We come to see that the ideal is to have enough to function effectively without the accumulation of things assuming an importance all out of proportion.

Don't try to deny your own personality in your effort to identify in your new culture. If we think we no longer appear foreign, we fool only ourselves. We need to ask God to use our differences, not annihilate them. Hang loose, work hard on that sense of humor and let God deal with discouragements and frustrations.

Time in Latin America doesn't mean what we've grown up thinking it does! Three o'clock can mean any time in the late afternoon. This will seem almost unchristian to you at times.

You may be thrown off guard if you expect effusive thanks or appreciation for help given or kindness done. Latins may be emotional but not in this way.

I am still wrestling with my Presbyterian attitudes toward truth and falsehood—all black and white with little room for the gray. Because of the importance of personal relationships here, this area can appear variable and cloudy. I am still trying to work through the psychological and Christian answers.

There is tremendous exhilaration in doing, with the Lord's help, things that would have seemed completely impossible at home. God gives the confidence that this stretching is from him and adds a satisfaction unmatched in our familiar and confident routine.

You'll be homesick sometimes but it will help to remember the restlessness of the long, gray winter months in the United States!

Your creative, cultural abilities will be needed here more than ever. Don't be afraid that you must leave them behind. The areas for expression may be less sophisticated but by the same token more individual and personal and perhaps even more satisfying. Edith Schaeffer's *Hidden Art* might be helpful in this area.

The very fact of starting to operate on a lower income than we're accustomed to in North America has its own special set of adjustments. Some will feel this more than others. Once upon a time life was cheap in developing countries, but that has changed radically and is something that seems very difficult for our friends in the North to grasp. "Missionary" still means "inexpensive." This is one area in which we need special grace from the Lord because its irritants attack us without warning.

I hope you will feel free to write if you have specific questions. The fact that I can think of so few problem areas shows how quickly the human animal adjusts to a new environment. These are just very personal reactions, but other friends helped me with theirs in the beginning.

Sincerely,
Lois

Letter 14

Paternalism

Dear John,

You seem to feel that in several letters I have inferred that North Americans are paternalistic and that this is a bad thing. You are right on both scores. Of course you are proud of our country and grateful for everything it has provided. I do not think the Lord intends any of us to be rootless even though "here we have no continuing city." Even Paul in his letter to a settlement of Roman army veterans wrote that he was a Pharisee of the tribe of Benjamin. God has given a particular identity to each of us which is part of our individuality, and he expects to use it.

Instead of replying directly let me explain myself. "Paternal" in a parent-child relationship is accurate and proper. But "paternalism" in an adult-adult relationship implies the bondage and suppression of the dependent one. I think we can say that paternalism between normal adults is always a violation of personality.

The point I want to make as strongly as I am able is that paternalism is not just a harmless attitude but a despicable curse. It is a denial of the integrity of the individual as a responsible person. It denies that the Holy Spirit is capable of transforming and developing anyone. The paternalistic person puts himself in the place of God. This attitude destroys the possibility of brethren being one in Christ because it infers that some have access to him and others need a go-between.

The classical examples of religious paternalism which have been studied exhaustively are found in the Jesuit Mission in Paraguay of the seventeenth century and the Franciscan Mission in California in the eighteenth. These missions were established without the use of force of any kind. By kindness and sacrifice on the part of missionary priests, the Indians in each place were persuaded to accept the new religion and adopt the basic elements of civilization in communal living under the supervision of the priests. They were fascinating experiments. The situation was idyllic in many ways. But the inevitable contact with European civilization and the loss of political power by the Jesuits and Franciscans made the result catastrophic. The Indians were completely unprepared to stand on their own feet and were left in worse condition than their original tribal culture. In Paraguay they have never recovered. In California they died out. Apart from the early years of a parent-child relationship (from which the word is derived), paternalism is always ultimately destructive.

We see ultimate paternalism in human slavery. The slave may be more comfortable than a free man, and he may be better fed. He may have more security but he is not free. But my concern is not only with the slave. The damage to the slave owner is incalculable. Did you ever look at North American paternalism in this light? Neither side can come out on top, but I would lay my bet for survival on national leaders. Paternalism robs us of the confidence that God can do what we cannot and gives us a built-in arrogance we cannot hide. We find that the most paternalistic students in the Language School are also the most pessimistic about the future of missions. They are beginning to realize their own helplessness.

I believe that we North Americans are congenitally paternalistic without being conscious of it. It is very difficult for us to see it in ourselves. Such statements may irritate North Americans. But the experience of most of us is that we simply cannot see this thing until we move into the other culture—and then only if we have the eyes to see. When you begin to see it for yourself, then there is hope.

Of course you simply consider yourself a North American who in his own culture has worked out a way of life that, theoretically at least, considers every person equal and free. I am not thinking of oppression or neglect, for these are matters which the blacks have developed eloquently, but of those relations which do not lead to violence. I am not questioning your honesty when you say you have "not an ounce of paternalism in my make-up."

One of our psychologists here states that paternalism results in acts which cannot be reciprocated. Put yourself in Latin America, in a slum or a rural area. How are you going to carry on your work in such a way that people will be able to reciprocate? Charity can become a curse which turns the receiver against the giver. Did you ever look at the golden rule in this light? After all, it is put positively by our Lord!

But put yourself with all your background in any place but upper-class Latin America. How can you erase the obvious differences? You have education. By comparison you are very wealthy. You have all your teeth and are in good health. You know how to get things done, and your knowledge of Scripture is encyclopedic. You eat regularly. Do you think these things do not show through? By any standard but the grace of God you have enormous advantages. You know and many nationals know the differences well. Day after day these differences will be driven home to you, and you will know your "superiority." And it will show.

Some national believers will be sufficiently mature to pray for you. Others will simply consider it one of the occupational diseases of North Americans. And don't forget that many believers have been conditioned by centuries of paternalism to expect you to act paternalistically. You not only have to be on your guard, but you have a deeply entrenched pattern to break. In addition to this, you will find some non-evangelicals who are sure this is one of the sins of Protestantism. You will be classed with the imperialists and the CIA. But spiritually the real problem is what this attitude will do to your own life. The believers will survive although their growth may be stunted, and you will be the one damaged. You can grow intolerant and cynical, and you can develop deep insecurity. Can you see why we are sensitive to this attitude? We can be so kindhearted, generous, willing or sympathetic that we sin against God and man. It is not easy to be a missionary. We are playing with fire —it can destroy us as well as warm us.

Paternalism is a dirty word in Latin America because it conjures up 150 years of being despised by Europeans and North Americans. If you want to know its implications, consider the terms associated with it: colonialism, exploitation, imperialism, landing of the Marines, occupation and second rate. Given the situation, your very presence as a foreigner implies to the evangelical church leaders that they cannot do the job and that you are here because you think you can. There is a saying: "Scratch a Latin and you will find an anti-American. Leave him alone and you will not see it."

We do not imply that Latins are more sensitive than North Americans. But our past behavior and our current attitudes indicate that we think we know what is best for the whole world. It is difficult for others to trust us as brothers in Christ. I have not exaggerated the problem. I hope I have not oversimplified it.

Another serious problem in connection with this paternalism is that most North American organizations, including missionary societies, look on overseas work in a more paternalistic manner than toward similar domestic activity. Secular society automatically considers overseas work a hardship post and so raises salaries, provides extra vacations, gives more travel allowance, provides special educational funds and handles many of the affairs of its employees in a way that would be resented in the United States. Naturally there are historical reasons for this, but when a missionary organization acts towards its missionaries in a paternalistic manner, how can these same missionaries avoid a paternalistic relationship with nationals? Is it any wonder we so often hear, "Missionary, go home!"

Let me end this rather gloomy letter with a suggestion as to how paternalism may be avoided. If you can look at the people around you, whether illiterate or educated, and from your heart can say to them, "You can do greater works than I am doing," then you are thinking of them as equals under the power of the Holy Spirit. Our Lord said exactly this and his cultural differential was far greater than ours.

Sincerely,
Charles

Letter 15

The Servant:
The Dedicated and
the Humorous

Dear John,

I am sorry that my letter on paternalism raised such grave questions in your mind about the possibility of effective service in Latin America. I want to make it very clear that this is not a problem you would have to face alone. It is common to all of us —Mexican, Argentinian, Canadian or those from the U.S.A. Like learning Spanish—there is no way out but through.

May I say that for most of us to watch ourselves being transformed from missionaries to servants is a very satisfying and profound experience. I hope you and your wife can have the excitement of discovering this same enrichment.

Let me also mention a note I have just come across that you may find helpful. About ten years ago at the Annual Meeting of a very large missionary society in Latin America, the United States headquarters proposed this question for discussion: "What personal characteristic is the most important for missionary effectiveness?" The Candidate Secretary wanted an on-the-spot evaluation of what kind of person he was to look for. He used this means of promoting interchange and of involving himself as an outsider in the thought processes of the workers. The question was discussed in several sessions, at meals, during breaks and on every possible occasion. It is interesting that the list was cut down to two: a sense of dedication and a sense of humor.

Sincerely,
Charles

Letter 16

The Priority of People

Dear John,

Your analysis of our personnel policy is very acute. You sense that we are playing down "the work of missions" in favor of the individual as a person. I have never put it quite so strongly. North Americans with their background of a technological culture naturally think of projects or areas in which people can be useful. The Latins put the thing delightfully in reverse. They think first of people and then of the possibility that they may be able to do something. The more I think of it, the more I feel you understand what we are trying to do.

There has been a reaction against the concept that "the work, the work" is the only thing that matters and that everything must be sacrificed for it. Though there is something attractive and romantic about such single-minded dedication and there are many brilliant examples of this, we do not often hear of the wreckage in broken relationships, neglected families, offended brethren, cynical children or frustrated followers. We have, in our single-mindedness, assumed that the concept of the absolute priority of God in our lives means that he pushes everything else out of the way that he has given us. To put God first does not exclude family and other relationships. They are very much a part of his plan for us.

Two quotations, both from contemporaries, have helped me see God's point of view in this matter. One from India, "God is more interested that you become like His Son than in anything you can do for Him." The other from Egypt, "It is easier for God to make a saint of a man with five children than of a bachelor." Actually such attitudes present a far more complex and strenuous approach to life than concentrating solely on "the work."

So you might describe us as a fellowship of people seeking to do certain things rather than as an organization promoting specific projects. But after all, what do North American Christians have to offer to the world but themselves? Advanced technology can come through a Moslem or Hindu. Special institutions anywhere in the world can be copied and adapted. What is it that we have to offer? More projects? More money? Actually we are like "one beggar telling another beggar where to find bread."

Sorry this sounds so much like a sermon, but we do feel keenly on this matter. It is in the context of biblical priorities that we say that the Community is more people-oriented than project-oriented.

Sincerely,
Charles

Letter 17

Ecumenism

Dear John,

Sooner or later I was expecting to receive your question on our understanding of the unity of the church. Your letter shows clearly that it came from North America because nowhere else would this question be phrased in quite the same way. In most of Europe where state churches dominate, plans for unity have unique characteristics. Even in a country like Australia which more closely resembles the situation you know the tensions and problems are very different. And in the Third World the situation is different again.

It is in this Third World that the Community serves. We make our decisions on the basis of what we see here and not on what we know of alignments in North America or Europe. You can imagine that this causes misunderstanding, but before God, in Latin America, we have no other choice. For example, a church in Michigan asked one of its missionaries in Honduras to state in writing his position on cooperation with Billy Graham. Continued support depended on the "correct" reply. This church could not see that the fact that Billy Graham had never preached in that country made this question and decision irrelevant so far as the work of Christ in that country was concerned.

Just recently I received a four-page questionnaire from a church which has provided part of our support. I had to leave many questions unanswered because in the context of the mission field, they had no meaning. For example: What is your attitude towards the Committee of Rehabilitation? Do you believe in soul life? Do you practice what the Bible teaches about length of hair? Do you insist on the separation of Church and State? And so the questions went on. This last one was particularly irrelevant because we serve in a country whose constitution clearly states that the "Holy Roman Catholic and Apostolic Church is the only recognized church and is the church of this country" (even though religious freedom is guaranteed). This country also has a concordat with the Vatican, and we have a Papal Nuncio in residence. I must not be too critical. These questions evidently represent important spiritual issues in Michigan, and I must not insist that our problems be theirs. Yet to us, this is a perfect example of an attempt to import North American issues into the church in Latin America.

Nevertheless, in spite of these differences between Latin and North America, we are solidly committed to the unity of the body of Christ around the world. This is not a matter of strategy or policy but of obedience to the Lord's commands. This means that no matter where we may find another brother in Christ, no matter how embarrassing or confusing his connections may be to us or ours to him, we are obligated to consider him a fellow member of the body of Christ and act accordingly.

In Latin America we find this ecumenical concept on several levels:

1. The organic union level. Recent events in several parts of the world point to less emphasis in this area in the future. It has never been a very serious issue in Latin America.

2. The project level. In countries with so much need, both Christian and secular groups find themselves interested in the same things—child care, drug abuse, freedom of assembly, religion and so forth.

3. A spiritual fellowship. A hunger for the Word of God, a desire for in-depth sharing, a common interest in pastoral de-

velopment, Sunday schools and literature programs bring people together from many groups who in North America and Europe would have quite different alignments.

4. The evangelistic level. It is here that our members have found the deepest expression of the unity of Christ's body. Evangelism-in-Depth has been the best public demonstration of this unity. We find in Latin America that the proclamation of the gospel is the finest opportunity to express unity in Christ, whether in the great year-long crusades or encounters in small groups.

5. The use of spiritual gifts. This is one of the most fruitful but most difficult levels on which we can express our unity in Christ. In so many traditional ecumenical discussions of past years, the vast diversity of God's operations seemed to have been ignored. Each cluster of gifts tended to be institutionalized, and thus outreach for Christ was compartmentalized. Those who stressed Bible teaching formed their own missions, evangelists formed their own and the same could be said for medical folk, charismatics or agriculturalists. We try to hold ourselves open to all these gifts for the building up of the body.

Now whether this analysis is applicable to the rest of the world, I do not know, but this is the situation here. We do not criticize other positions although we may not understand them. Nor do we insist that our insights are valid for all other situations, but we do pray that North Americans will not try to impose their systems here.

The difference of this openness will strike you first in the wide variety of worship services you will have contact with. You would have to be a church tramp in the United States to find a comparable variety. I imagine your own preference is for a quiet, formal style of worship, but as a missionary you will be faced with other forms. We hope you will be open both psychologically and spiritually. I know you are open theologically.

Some believers find deep, transforming experiences of

Christ in liturgical services which may appear anachronistic or theatrical to you. There are formal services which may make you wonder whether anything from the spiritual world has been communicated. And then there are services so informal that you will wonder whether anything is going on at all. Others will strike you as sheer entertainment. And in some there is an unimaginable din which leaves your ears ringing. Some services consist mostly of singing. Can you clap for two hours of hymn singing? There are some very long sermons, and you will learn to pray out loud with the whole congregation. And prayer meetings! It is not uncommon for them to go on all night, and none fit any regular time schedule. In many of the public as well as private meetings the believers simply expect God to heal those for whom they pray. There is no demanding that he perform a miracle. It is just that he has told them to pray for the sick—they do and some are healed.

It is not a question of whether you like these expressions of worship. The Holy Spirit is leading believers here in a wide variety of ways. It provides rich experiences although they can be harrowing! I have described these differences because I feel they express the sense of ecumenism or the unity and diversity of the body of Christ in Latin America better than do the categories with which you are familiar in North America.

On any mission field it is absolutely necessary to understand the decision-making processes in order that an individual's decision to accept Christ may have the stamp of reality. For example, several years ago a North American evangelist using an interpreter held a series of meetings in Latin America. Fantastic results were reported in Christian periodicals. Actually, Latin courtesy was such that when very few people responded to the preacher's extended invitations, the whole congregation went forward night after night. They felt sorry for such an important and sincere visitor and saw that this action gave him great satisfaction. And I have heard exactly the same thing in

Taiwan. We must understand how people respond before we count hands.

We are conscious that God has placed us in a country whose people react very differently from our own. As you know, statistics are very unreliable in this part of the world, partly because most Christians do not consider them important but also because criteria differ so widely. Yet missionaries who are acquainted with the whole of Latin America describe the situation in ways that confirm our own experience. Their general observations pose very important questions for North Americans:

1. Pentecostal denominations are growing ten times faster than mission churches of main-line denominations and five times faster than churches of independent "faith" missions. *What is the difference between the direct work of the Holy Spirit and the natural response of Latin culture and temperament to mounting unrest and tension?*

2. In many places there are more conversions to Christ in Roman Catholic churches than through those of evangelical missions. *What should our attitude be toward those who feel they are called to remain in their own church?*

3. Three quarters of Latin evangelical Protestants, regardless of denomination, consider themselves charismatic, exercising various types of gifts of the Spirit, some dramatic, some unspectacular. *What does this mean in the training of new North American missionaries?*

4. Half the evangelical Christians, some say three quarters, hold political views which by U.S. standards are far to the left. *Will North American evangelical churches continue to support Latin American evangelism in the face of this?*

5. Ninety-five per cent of Protestant missionaries coming to Latin America are conservative evangelicals. *How are they to act given the make-up of the churches in Latin America?*

This is completely unlike anything we have known before,

and we are often baffled at God's unexpected ways of working. Yet we rejoice with Latin American believers at the openness and the opportunities for the gospel which this part of the world has never known before.

Yet how do we maintain doctrinal faithfulness? Each year all missionaries are required to state in writing their agreement with our Basis of Faith. You have already received these papers.

I do not need to tell you that this method is not always adequate. You know the situation in your own denomination where the solemn ordination vow to uphold your confession often seems to be insufficient. It is a question of personal conscience. The Mission does not have a committee to review doctrinal integrity. You see our problem is not whether candidates, like yourself, are in theological agreement with our doctrinal basis—the Board of Trustees takes care of that—but whether we continue to grow in our theological understanding and still remain biblical.

We would be deeply disappointed if after ten years your grasp of theology remained at the same level as at the present moment. The natural progress of growing experience, of facing the situations of another culture, of raising teen-agers and of facing new problems you cannot now anticipate should drive your theological comprehension deeper as well as wider. Have you worked out a theology of sex for new believers in a situation where both men and women may have had three spouses and three families, two of which may be existing side by side? Or a theology of political action? Or of economic oppression and inequality? My guess is that you have had neither the opportunity nor the need to develop any of these.

Our responsibility is to face North American theological issues as North Americans without necessarily importing them into Latin America. We must also face the live issues here and face them "according to the Scriptures." With your training you know how difficult this is. Most heresies have grown with the very best of intentions.

One of our solutions is to provide discussions, seminars and study groups among ourselves in a spirit of open confidence in order to check and encourage one another. Naturally the seminary faculty members are most directly engaged in this activity, but it is for the sake of all of us. Since we are all fallible and prone to error, this is a work of grace that is occasionally humiliating.

You may come from a background where legal measures are set up to maintain doctrinal integrity and may find this informal way unsatisfactory. But faithfulness to the Scriptures is a very personal matter, and we pray for one another in dependence on the Holy Spirit. Actually, we find that with evangelism as our major thrust, this involvement in bringing men and women to Christ is one of God's means of keeping us in the Word.

Sincerely,
Charles

Letter 18

The Roman Catholic Church

Dear John,

We need to be reminded that North Americans tend to lump all of Latin America together. I probably have done so in my letters, and I am certain that you have read me that way. But this is far from the truth. At first glance the common languages and history (Spanish-Portuguese) are deceptive. A little travel will show the fallacy. Even in the tiny Banana Republics of Central America, the cities of Managua, San José and Panama have different histories, governments and attitudes. I once heard a Colombian say that Mexico resembles the United States far more than it does Colombia. It would be violently disputed by a Mexican, but it illustrates the point that Latins can be foreigners in Latin America. And even in a single city there is wide diversity, especially in religious attitudes which cover everything from medievalism to Catholic charismatics and all stages between.

It is with this in mind that I answer your very specific question, "What is your attitude toward the Roman Catholic Church?" From one perspective this question is answered for us. The government in many countries officially establishing the Roman Church has settled the matter for us legally. Since Vatican II, according to the church itself, Protestants are "separated brethren" who have some validity as part of the body of Christ but who should ideally be under the Papal See. Some bishops have forgotten what was said in Rome and still seem to classify us as heretics. It is also an integral part of the culture, counting over ninety-five per cent of the population as members.

Practically though, this means that Protestants are no longer arch enemies to be avoided at all costs, at least where the hierarchy has gone along with the Vatican Council. You can imagine what differences this has made for evangelicals. We are watching this tremendous flux within the Roman Church. Evangelicals have contact now with many, many Catholic laymen, priests, nuns and members of the hierarchy. Many of those who have come into what they call an "evangelical experience of authentic Christianity" have not left the Roman Church. For many reasons we as evangelicals do not feel that we have the right to insist that these new believers exchange their church for ours.

Now with my Protestant background this produces a number of hangups—but they are mine and not theirs. I have not fully resolved the theological implications in my own mind except to be convinced that, at the moment, these new believers are not cowards, traitors to the gospel or incompetents.

This situation means that we as missionaries and foreigners will take all the opportunities we can to study, discuss, witness and pray with Roman Catholics whenever they are willing and wherever they may be found. And that may be in parochial schools, universities, homes, convents, churches or seminaries. We do not see all the implications of this witnessing but it is the path of obedience.

This morning at coffee break—a very sacred institution in a coffee producing country—I discussed the Community's attitude to the Roman Church with some of my colleagues. Certainly we are not sitting on the sidelines waiting for the established church to become Protestant so that we can say that we were right all the time, but my colleagues felt that what I have said so far is only a partial description of the situation.

Remember this is Latin America with its centuries of feudalistic tradition and revolutionary activities. Some of us feel that we are living in an era comparable to the period between the Renaissance and Reformation when all kinds of movements and ideas were in the air. Some of them coalesced in northern Europe in the Reformation. We do not expect a repetition here, but the interest in the renewal of the church is similar. At this moment we have no idea what the decisive events may be. Who would have thought that the Reformation could have been triggered by a German monk or a king who wanted a male heir?

In Latin America we are seeing the Spirit of God at work in all levels of Roman Catholic and Protestant churches in ways we would have considered impossible even fifteen years ago. He did not consult us nor ask our permission nor has he always involved us. Certainly we can take no credit. You can appreciate the confusion of many evangelicals who have been at the receiving end of Catholic persecution and discrimination all of their lives. Let me just list some encounters which have awakened us to this new work of God.

A Colombian priest who had led in the persecution of evangelicals personally asked the pardon of the Church Association leaders.

We are asked to sell New Testaments after services in any number of Catholic churches. On several occasions the priest has called the evangelicals to the altar rail, blessed their efforts, identified with them in Bible reading and urged the faithful to buy copies after mass. It is difficult to keep a sufficient supply on hand.

Evangelical student workers are asked to assist in retreats for Catholic students. We apparently are considered experts in "how to study the Bible" and "how to decide for Christ."

We have long since lost count of the prayer groups and Bible studies that include Roman Catholics and Protestants.

A priest who led a radio home Bible study hour was so inundated with requests for help that he recommended they seek out local evangelicals to help lead the groups because "evangelicals know the Bible."

One of my friends visited a local Sunday evening mass and remarked, "I would like to have given exactly the same message. It sounded just like Billy Graham."

More amazing still, there are Roman Catholic priests who have brought spiritual revival to evangelical churches!

It is not surprising that we see this movement with special clarity in student work. Just a few months ago a student worker led twenty-two students to Christ at a Roman Catholic retreat; at an evangelical university camp, a priest led some thirty to put their trust in Christ.

We are well aware that there are theological and ecclesiastical problems, but we cannot deny that in these face-to-face encounters we see the work of the same Spirit who brought us into the "fellowship of his Son." I do not know how this compares with your experience in the eastern United States, but this is what we see happening here. At the same time the old conservative Catholic attitudes continue in many places side by side with these new winds of the Spirit.

We hope that you will join us in this confused but wonderful situation.

Sincerely,
Charles

Letter 19

Communism

Dear John,

Your next question was inevitable and I was expecting it: "What is the Community's attitude towards communism?" This is a very natural question, and I am going to reply with a question: "What kind of communism? Cuban? Chinese? Russian? 'Christian'? or Chilean?" And I am not joking. You see, your problem seems to recognize only two ideologies: a capitalism that is already strongly socialistic or a communism that is already imperialistic. In Latin America the only real capitalism is that found in the great landed estates (which is really feudalism) or the exploitation by international industries. Otherwise, even in colonial times, the governments have always been the active agents in the economy. They are the only bodies with enough resources to do anything.

So you see, in Latin America, the choice really lies only within the broad spectrum of socialism—from government control and ownership of major sectors only to absolute, centralized control of everything. It is not a simple choice of one type of socialism over another, but a recognition of a dynamic, changing situation. In fact revolution is in the air. I don't know how you react to this word, but it is very respectable here—like the word "democracy" in the United States.

There is general agreement here that the whole structure of society must be changed. For those on the top of the present heap the problem is how to live through a revolution and still stay on top. For those with nothing the problem is how to wrest control. For those with a Christian orientation the problem is how to bring in justice without violence and bloodshed. Latin America is not unusual. It is only an aggravated case of the inadequacy of the structure of all society to handle present tensions.

You will see this more clearly if you come to live here. I have tried to be realistic not to urge you to bring a solution with you but to prepare you psychologically. I do not know your political persuasion, but if you are what is called a convinced right-wing citizen, then you are headed for emotional turmoil in trying to serve in a revolutionary society. I do not want to close the door, but I say this because some missionaries find they cannot adjust.

So your question does not have one simple answer. You will find a variety of political opinions among us. The real question at this point is whether you feel that you and your family are willing to try to live as Christians in a revolutionary society. If you are you are most welcome. But communism, however you define it, is not the only option.

Sincerely,
Charles

Letter 20

Raising Support

Dear John,

I gather that you are bothered by the prospect of having to raise your support. I don't blame you. Lois and I almost did not come because of this issue. We could not bring ourselves to beg for our support. Perhaps we were too proud, but I think at heart we resented the attitude of some churches, pastors and friends who have a double standard for themselves and their missionary family. I was used to raising money for Christian groups, so the fact itself did not bother me. But to adopt the position of beggar before the opulent was awfully hard to take. Praise God, there were those who by their enthusiasm and sacrifice let us know that we were fellow workers.

Now this business of raising your own support has a venerable history. It was first used when there were so many candidates that an additional method had to be devised to screen those who could not communicate sufficiently. After World War I this system presupposed a church, Bible Institute, Christian College, Seminary sequence of training which gave the candidate a host of friends and church connections who expected to support overseas candidates. You have not come up this way, nor, as a matter of fact, do many of today's candidates.

Consequently, our policy is to make support-raising a joint effort. The presence of Latin missionaries who have no personal access to areas of possible support in the United States or elsewhere makes this imperative. The main office in the United States will work with you from the beginning. You will decide to go alone to make some contacts. You and the office will work together for others. This provides experienced counsel. You are not entirely alone.

As you are able to cut through the dependency syndrome, you will see the Christian authority for your "begging." Whether your potential donors realize it or not, God is giving them a chance to work overseas by proxy. It is a rare privilege because, since they cannot go themselves, through you they have their opportunity. The Lord is giving them this as one road to obedience. You are his instrument to bring this about. I know that the term "personal support" clouds the issue, but there is no other adequate word. But more important than any of these considerations is the fact that we have the highest authority for this dependency. Our Lord was maintained in his physical needs by the service and support of a few wealthy women as we are told in Luke 8:3. Let's not place ourselves above him.

The chief advantage of doing your own deputation lies in the individual contacts which will establish your base not just of support but of prayer. At times you will sense that the prayers of these friends are the only thing between you and collapse. You will want a body of friends to whom you may direct special requests. In other words you will need a broad base of backers. The best time for this preparation is before leaving the United States initially. You will have this advantage only once. Tackle it with enthusiasm and take time to lay a solid foundation. This two-way ministry also means giving your friends a deeper understanding of the Christian life and the gospel than they could gain in Pennsylvania alone. You will broaden their horizons, communicate new perspectives, help them grasp the meaning of sharing, enlarge their vision and produce an intelligent missionary concern. We place a good deal of emphasis on this ministry to our supporting friends.

Don't be in such a hurry to get here that you leave with a minimum number. When you are on location, you will have only newsletters to keep communication open. Unless you are a Shakespeare you will find these letters only very feeble signals if the recipients do not know your face and have only a very faint memory of your ministry to them.

Some of our Latin coworkers see this matter of raising their support from a different viewpoint. Since most of these leaders have been employed by various missions, it is bewildering to them to try to grasp the North American idea of raising personal support. Imagine how you would feel if you were required to raise your support in Brazil! After a long session with a Latin who had applied to the Mission, I felt unable to make this policy clear. "Since the Mission has employed me these years, why can't it continue to do so?" A logical question, but hard to answer. Finally he said, "I think I see. If I am to have the same standing as a North American missionary and not be just a national employee, and if I am to be treated like a professional, then I must be self-supporting by raising my own support."

Sincerely,
Charles

Letter 21

Racism

Dear John,

I am especially glad for your last question. It is unusual for a candidate to request information on the Community's position on race. This may be for several reasons. I think most North American Christians would feel that the matter had been settled by the very existence of missions. In a sense this is true. Missions have a heroic record of opposing racism or, more positively, of demonstrating God's love to all men. In this part of the world Bartoleme de Las Casas with the Indians and San Pedro Claver among African slaves are the great missionary-priest figures under Spanish colonialism. As recently as 150 years ago in England it was Christian missionaries who stood against the scientific attitudes of that day which could "prove" that Africans were subhuman and Asians were incapable of development equal to that of the West. Our missionary heritage is a magnificent one!

Still the modern missionary faces a very complex problem. Let me see whether I can describe it. I know of no mission society which is racist either officially or in practice although some of their members may have racist attitudes. There may be an exception to this statement in the prohibition by some missions against marrying nationals. Of course other reasons are given, but they do not sound very convincing.

Yet because the issues which reflect racism vary from country to country, those who do not recognize the symptoms often condone (or do not see) practices that are racist. For example most black Costa Ricans feel that they have a better chance of freedom and personal advancement in the United States than here. Yet when North American blacks come to Costa Rica, they feel that at last they have found a racist-free country.

How can we explain this? I think it is that the expressions of racism in one culture are not the same in another. A person who is discriminated against in his own country knows the frustrations of his own culture. When he finds himself outside this particular situation, he senses a tremendous freedom. The discriminatory practices of the new country do not seem to have the same emotional impact. We seldom sense any discrimination when we first move into a different culture. Our problem as missionaries is that, not seeing them, we may unconsciously adopt racist practices.

We North Americans flagellate ourselves over black-white racism. We can be so sensitive to our own situation that we fail to realize that racism is not a North American monopoly. Let's face it! The whole world is racist but each culture in its own way. In Latin America there is a four-way possibility for trouble—white, Indian, black, Oriental. Because of the fact that inter-racial marriage is more common here than in the North, a North American may conclude that racism does not exist. In the United States sense it may not, but in Latin America the mere color of the skin often has more to do with marriage and employment than other factors. Or in another area, while no discriminatory laws are on the books, it is still very, very difficult for a black or an Indian to obtain a responsible position though qualified.

I do not think any mission society can guarantee that it is completely free of racism. The best that can be done is to take an organizational and biblical stance against it and then pray that when racist attitudes are exposed, each person will have the wisdom to settle them with integrity. You will find very few missionaries who show any overt racism. We can be thankful for this. Probably the crucial test will come when your teen-age daughter falls in love with a Latin! And by then I trust you will have grown to the place where you can see her as a person rather than as an ethnic symbol.

Sincerely,
Charles

Letter 22

Church Planting

Dear John,

I see you have been influenced by one school of thought which makes the purpose of mission societies chiefly that of "church planting." Now I don't want to take issue here because I am in almost total agreement, but I do feel that when our Lord spoke of us as "light" and "salt" he was thinking of more than planting churches. He has a concern also for "man in society." For many generations we have seen too much of a church interested only in itself, in this part of the world, and one not interested enough in the whole of God's creation.

In writing this I do not want to downgrade the work of church planting. It is still a major objective in most missionary societies and one aspect of our work. Some are specifically called to this work and from time to time church planting becomes the major activity of missionaries whose major responsibility lies elsewhere. What I am objecting to is forcing all personnel into one activity and declaring that this is the only reason for service. By so doing we deny the variety of the gifts of the Spirit.

But the question you face is not the "mission of the Mission" but the mission of John, a thirty-year-old North American, a highly educated foreigner. What are you going to do? As I have written before, with few exceptions church planting can be done better by national pastors and evangelists than by a foreigner. Increasingly many other tasks can be handled better in this way. It is here that we may jump to the wrong conclusion that foreigners are no longer usable.

All that I have written so far could be summed up sociologically by saying that a foreigner here has his best opportunity by entering existing institutions to serve and carry out his witness. You did not form your own denomination to be able to preach. A doctor need not build his own hospital in order to work as a Christian doctor. There are already churches and Christian organizations in Latin America, and increasingly secular institutions are opening for the services of foreign Christians.

There was a time not long ago when secular institutions were closed to evangelicals, and there were few churches or Christian organizations. But this has changed. One missionary has been a member of the government Planning Commission, another a Minister of Education, another a director of a Public Health Clinic, another is teaching religion in a local high school, another teaches swimming. The penetration of areas normally closed to evangelicals is being carried out effectively, and the impact of the growth on the churches is incalculable. This could possibly be the most significant area of missionary evangelism in the future. We must not dismiss this possibility simply because it is so different from the past.

This principle is particularly important for professionals because it opens a lifelong opportunity for service in the country of adoption.

Sincerely,
Charles

Letter 23

Professional Mobility

Dear John,

You are still wrestling with what you see as a conflict between the concept of a "professional" and my description of exploding opportunities with their potential for new activities. "Forced into work" was the way you put it. This reaction comes straight out of the contemporary North American culture. A Latin American would never feel this way nor would your grandfather. It is a product of modern industrialization and management plus the attitude of our educational establishment that a diploma certifies qualification. You see what this means. It implies that you do nothing for which you have not had the proper training. A manager at Grade IV level is where he is because he has had the Grade IV training course and is working toward the next level.

This may be a possible mode of life in a sophisticated industrial society, but Latin America is in the process of a different development. In any situation where your work is growing, you will be "forced" into positions of service for which you are not formally prepared. The only way to avoid this situation is to stop growing. In missionary work this is not an option.

It is perfectly true that many missionaries are doing work for which they had no training. This is seldom the fault of the arbitrary or sadistic tendencies of administrators, but the result of sheer necessity or, better still, of exploding opportunities. A friend of mine came to Latin America as maintenance man for a mission, became head of a Bible school and is now spearheading an agricultural extension program for pre-evangelism. He has done an excellent job in each spot. In each instance he responded to a need, gladly and willingly. Such men educate themselves in their new work—the hard way.

I am not writing about emergencies. In case of sickness, death or any sudden, unavoidable change of plans, any of us is willing to pitch in and do what we can. I know you were not thinking of this type of thing but rather of what may appear an unreasonable pressure which would not take into account your own feelings or qualifications, simply that of filling a slot.

Let me add two personal observations. The first is the great number of people in middle age who feel they are trapped in a rut. So many of my college friends complain of the frustration of their work. In the early days of professional life they had all the excitement of beginning a significant career. Now, although most are very successful, it is the same old grind. And they have another fifteen years of it before retirement! By the very nature of the case, missionary life is not like this. In fact sometimes we long for a little rut!

The second factor is your own personal development. Modern vocational counseling can be misapplied in such a way that we box ourselves in at an early age feeling we know what our interests and capabilities are. Some of us are late bloomers. Most of us do not know what latent abilities we have until we are forced into situations not of our own choosing. What Scotsman would have thought that the shy young Mary Slessor, who had gone to assist a missionary in Africa, would show uncanny ability to gain the confidence of cannibal chiefs? Fortunately for the work of Christ in Africa, Scotland offered no opportunity to develop this talent. Your own growth in character and spiritual depth ought not to be circumscribed in advance. The Lord knows where he is taking you and will be there ahead of you.

However, I think I can understand your concern. I can only assure you that every position is filled here with the full concurrence of all parties concerned. The important thing is not to confine your interest to areas of past experience or vocational testing only but to commit yourself to the hands of One who knows you as no other. You can be very confident that the gifts of the Holy Spirit are given liberally to those who need them. And I think that even from a selfish point of view this attitude of openness to the Lord will lead you into a more interesting and valuable life than you could possibly plan for yourself.

Sincerely,
Charles

Letter 24

Dropouts

Dear John,

I am not surprised that one of your fellow pastors feels that missions are for dropouts. I am afraid that this feeling is more general than we like to admit. Last night I was with a group of churchy North Americans who were sounding off about missionaries. With the Language Institute here in San José they have plenty of exposure. As usual the only missionaries they noticed were the really odd characters whose strange attitudes they assumed to be typical. Of course I egged them on. One man later nearly swallowed his coffee cup when I told him that two of us in the group were missionaries. I do not think that they believed us when we told them that among the 165 Language School students this term there were two doctors, seven nurses, two Ph.D's, seven engineers, to say nothing of the large number of BD's, M.Th's, D.Th's and MRE's. But of course they were thinking only of the "dropout" type.

Let's look at this objectively. A majority of people mature most effectively outside their early environment. A prophet has honor except in his home town. After all, the Lord had a rough time in Nazareth. Now we recognize this in vocational guidance and in the placement of pastors and teachers. We know that the average person has a better chance of success if he does not return home. This is in no sense being a dropout. This carries no derogatory overtones. Yet somehow with missionaries who leave their own countries these overtones exist.

Interestingly enough we find men who are real dropouts in the business and diplomatic community. Many of them are doing better here than they could have done in the United States or Canada. Novelists have developed this theme. Yet why is it that such a business man or engineer is considered an interesting adventurer while a missionary is a dropout?

While it is true that some people find a more satisfactory and effective niche in another culture, the tremendous demands of missionary life make it dangerous to use this factor as guidance. In this part of the world you will always feel unprepared whatever you do. You will need more theology than you have, more psychology, more sociology, more anthropology. You will want more training in education, counseling or management. You will never have enough preparation. To hope that you may be more productive here simply because you are overseas shows a serious lack of understanding the role of the missionary.

You may feel that you have a better chance to develop your own character in this culture than where you are now. The Lord in his loving wisdom may be leading you along this path, but be very sure. If this is a device to escape this development in North America, it is only a more personal form of a real dropout attitude. The statistics would be against you. About one-third of the missionaries who go through Language School do not return to their fields after their first term. Of course there are many reasons, but an inability to cope with their bicultural situation stands high on the list.

Do try to erase from your mind the thought that you are coming to a second-class situation in which you will have an advantage over the "natives." It is just the opposite.

Sincerely,
Charles

Letter **25**

Real Missionary Work

Dear John,

Your last letter was so full of questions that I wonder whether you are approaching a decision. They fall into four groups and the answers may surprise you.

What extra preparation do I need? Your personal desires, your own qualifications as well as your temperament all enter into the matter. Since you are thinking in terms of some form of pastoral work, I would suggest that you get some good sociology. Most missionaries find extra study more valuable after a time on the field.

How can I be sure of God's call? I dare not answer this by letter. This is such a personal matter. I suggest that after thorough discussions with your wife, you then seek the counsel and prayer fellowship of other Christians. The Lord has his own ways of showing his will and no one else can do it for you.

Am I physically up to mission life? The answer is probably yes. If you can survive the rigors of a Northeastern winter, you are good material. But this is basically a medical problem. You may not be able to take the extreme tropics or very high altitudes, but most people find they can adapt to everything in between.

In answer to your other questions, let me just summarize— we can be specific later on. Life here may be more similar to North America than you expect. Apart from the language and some customs, there would probably be as much difference in leaving Manhattan, say, for Eastern Kentucky as in coming here. After all, except for the Indian areas we are a part of Western European culture. Think in terms of joining a home mission society to work in a needy area. If you went to northern Arizona or central Montana there would be certain living conditions that you would find different from Philadelphia though not drastically so. Our visitors who want to see "real missionary work," in exotic, isolated, thatched-roof locations, indicate that they find many Latin cities so like North America that they discount them as missionary centers. The "pith helmet" mentality of some North American visitors is no joking matter for missionaries on the field. One visitor, a pastor who had been a strong friend of missions for many years, finally made his first visit to the Latin American field. The missionaries were most gracious with time and effort to show him every aspect of the work so that he could understand principles, methods and results. He was shown medical and educational work, children and student ministries, rural relief, church planting and evangelism in the area surrounding the capitol city where eighty per cent of the people live. At the end of a three-day visit he said, "And now I am ready to see *real* missionary work!"

Another visitor remarked, "Why do you all live in the city? How can you be missionaries?" There was an inability to understand that missionaries go where the people are and in Latin America this means cities for the most part. In Brazil there are more foreign missionaries per person in the Amazon valley than in the overcrowded cities of this great country.

A musical group from the United States came to help the churches for several weeks. It was possible because of school schedules to get them into high school assemblies. As a result some ten thousand students heard a Christian testimony for the first time. It was a unique breakthrough. It also so happened that the visitors were free to go with one missionary to a country baptismal service, two hours away by bus and two more on foot. Six believers were baptized in a muddy pool covered with green scum. In arranging for a subsequent tour, the director wrote, "This time we would prefer to spend our time ministering in missionary situations such as we did last year at the baptism."

Sincerely,
Charles

Letter 26

Immigration and Spiritual Battles

Dear John,

Although I am not advocating missionary work by immigration, this is one option. And why should you react so negatively to this? It is one of the oldest forms for the extension of the gospel. The early Moravians practiced it extensively, and we can also include the Pilgrim Fathers and the Spanish colonists in the New World.

I realize that immigration may not be open in some parts of the world, but it certainly is in Latin America. China and India are overpopulated and Africa is not interested, but many countries down this way encourage it. In fact in the last 150 years since independence from Spain, hundreds of thousands of Europeans and North Americans have voluntarily made their homes here. O'Higgins was a liberator of Chile, Levingston a president of Argentina and Keith a business man of Costa Rica.

The incongruity does not lie in their immigration but in the fact that the men and women most concerned for the spiritual well-being of Latin Americans seldom make this their home. They work for a few years, take long vacations in the North and then retire there. And yet there are thousands of others today with no higher motive than easy money who are prepared to call their adopted countries their own. Is it any wonder that missionaries are often not taken seriously or that students so often point out this inconsistency?

Canada and the United States are new countries, and the

natural pride which its citizens have in their culture and achievements must not be down-graded. But is United States citizenship so valuable a thing in comparison with the gospel? Could it interfere with your ability to obey the Great Commission? Now you may never have to choose between your own country and the country in which you serve. A mission society that insisted on immigration would be very unrealistic at the moment. Nor in writing this way do I share the current attitude of many who despise their native land. You yourself are proud of your Scottish ancestry although you are a citizen of the United States of America. Is there any reason why your children as Colombians or Costa Ricans could not be as proud of their Scottish-American background? My question is directed to your attitude toward the priorities of your life as you seek his guidance. Missionary service is not just an adventure but the serious business of obedience. The high calling of God transcends all earthly citizenships.

I also sympathize with your concern that I have avoided those "great spiritual issues of prayer, personal work, the victorious Christian life, holiness and the Lord's return" in connection with your missionary call. You must admit that any one of these subjects is more than enough for a book, certainly more than can be handled by correspondence between busy people. I have avoided dealing with these subjects deliberately although I hope I have never implied that they were not important.

You have mentioned God's pressuring you through times of prayer, missionary conferences and biographies as well as spiritual retreats. I know that statistics show that these activities are God's normal means of interesting folk in going overseas. But I am keenly aware that most young people moved even to the point of volunteering never get overseas except as tourists. But for those who go a spiritual idealism is not enough to get them through their first term.

What I have been trying to do is to help you develop that "something more" which will stand you in good stead when the inspiration of a missionary address and your response may seem very unreal. I have tried to do this by being as accurate as possible about the situation you may move into and then to look into your background, the Scriptures, your own inner life and your present pastorate to see whether the Lord might be leading in this direction. You have done this, and I have been strengthened personally by your sharing of the Lord's ways in your life.

There is a wrestling with principalities and powers which overshadows all matters of professional attitudes, language or bicultural experience. In our native culture we often become insensitive to this struggle, but somehow to live and work in another culture opens our eyes to the warfare. It is just here that the images of soldiers, battle and enemy apply. A popular phrase of World War II was, "The battle is the payoff." No intensity of call or vision, no perfection of training and maneuvers are of any value unless they are successful in battle. All this is so you may respond to God's call *and* stand in the battle. I wish it were possible for you to visit us and see all this for yourselves.

Sincerely,
Charles

Letter 27

The Issues

Dear Charles,

Carolyn and I want to express our deep gratitude for your Christian hospitality and time last week. This visit was certainly one of the greatest experiences of our lives. We shall never be the same.

Now that we are home again it is hard to reconstruct our pre-visit ideas. Just what did we expect? We found missionary work infinitely more challenging and complex than we thought . . . and this in spite of your pointing out that the part of Latin America we saw has more similarities to our own country than many other areas of the continent.

We really were not prepared for the great consequences of working in another language and culture and what it means to obey Jesus Christ under those circumstances. We have reread some of your letters which now take on completely new meanings. You had told us, but we understood so little.

I am afraid I expected to enjoy a year of study in the Language Institute and then step again into my role of ministry. I know you had warned us, but I underestimated the language barrier. Since I have studied French and German, I assumed that pastoral work in Spanish would come quickly. It did not occur to me that I could never have become a pastor-counselor in Paris or Berlin with my present knowledge of French or German. I suppose I could preach simple sermons at the end of language study, but as I looked into faces of that San José congregation, I realized that I would need a long learning experience before I could even listen to them, much less open up the Scriptures. I must confess that the thought of taking even a few years out of my ministry at this point to change cultural and linguistic gears has put our missionary interest in a new light. We do not feel that we have yet accurately counted this cost.

We tried to imagine the culture becoming our own rather than looking at it as tourists enjoying its quaintness. Certainly we had anticipated certain adjustments for communications purposes but had not thought much further. The service on Sunday evening was very lively and would terrify my own congregation, but I felt that with practice I could easily become part of it. But the afternoon with the student group showed us the real issues. They were genuine Christians. There was no doubt about that. But their attitudes toward everything we talked about were so very different from ours. Their comments on the churches, sex, politics, family life, economics, university life, everything reflected their different culture. In trying to analyze the strong reaction both of us had, we decided that what we were expecting was that ultimately, as a result of our ministry, Latin Americans would come to share not only our Savior, but our own North American attitudes as well. Here were students who were well on the way to Christian maturity who had no intention or desire to become like us.

Please do not misunderstand us. We are not judging what we saw. Of course, certain things puzzled us—things were not better or worse, just different. But we suddenly realized that our children would grow up more Latin than North American. And to them, all this would be normal. Their roots and ours would be in different cultures.

We suddenly began to realize the high degree of transfer we would have to make. I use this word rather than "having to give up" because it has no negative overtones. I believe that in theory we are ready to transfer (give up) anything for Christ's sake, but we have seen for the first time that these changes must be on our part.

For all these reasons we are going to take more time to think and pray through the issues as we now see them. We are conscious of a greater need and an urgency which we did not feel before, but at the same time we see ourselves with our cultural baggage and hangups in a new light. We are praying that the Lord will make his will known to us. The new thing which he has done since our visit with you is to give us a settled confidence that if his place for us is the mission field, he will make us usable in spite of ourselves.

Pray for us!

In his fellowship,
John and Carolyn